On Reading the Constitution

On Reading
the Constitution

Laurence H. Tribe
& Michael C. Dorf

HARVARD UNIVERSITY PRESS

Cambridge, Massachusetts, and London, England

1991

An earlier version of Chapters 1 and 2 originally appeared in the *Tanner Lectures on Human Values*, vol. 9, reprinted by permission of the University of Utah Press.

This book is printed on acid-free paper, and its binding materials have been chosen for strength and durability.

Library of Congress Cataloging-in-Publication Data
Tribe, Laurence H.
On reading the Constitution / Laurence H. Tribe and Michael C. Dorf.
p.   cm.
Includes bibliographical references and index.
ISBN 0-674-63625-2 (alk. paper)
1. United States—Constitutional law—Interpretation and construction.
I. Dorf, Michael C.   II. Title.
KF4550.T787   1991
342.73'02—dc20
[347.3022]   90-47064
CIP

For Polia Tribe and the memory of George Tribe,

and for Annette and Stanley Dorf

Acknowledgments

THIS BOOK DRAWS heavily on two previous works. The first of those works, "On Reading the Constitution," appeared in the *Utah Law Review* in 1988. It was a lightly edited version of the Tanner Lectures given by Laurence Tribe at the University of Utah in November 1986, and forms the basis for what became Chapters 1 and 2 of this book. Chapters 3 through 5 are based on "Levels of Generality in the Definition of Rights," a recent collaboration by the two of us, which first appeared in the Fall 1990 edition of the *Chicago Law Review*.

We are grateful for the outstanding efforts of several very talented people. Ken Chesebro was instrumental in transforming the Tanner Lectures into the *Utah Law Review* article. Shawn Martin and Julius Genachowski both provided invaluable research and analytical assistance in updating and revising that article for the book. Robert Fisher and Barrack Obama have influenced our thinking on virtually every subject discussed in these pages. Sherry Colb, Matthew Kreeger, and Peter Rubin gave constructive advice (especially to Michael Dorf) at every stage of this project.

We would also like to acknowledge the insights of all of the Harvard Law students in Laurence Tribe's Constitutional Law classes during the last five years, and especially those students in the Privacy class and the Advanced Constitutional Law Seminar during the spring of 1990.

Finally, we are grateful to Aida Donald and Harvard University Press for their patience and cooperation.

Contents

On Reading the Constitution

Introduction

IN A SPEECH delivered in 1984 at the University of San Diego, Justice Stevens of the United States Supreme Court remarked that "[t]he Constitution of the United States is a mysterious document."[1] What prompted Justice Stevens to take this view? A cynic might imagine that he sought to enhance his own power as a justice of the Supreme Court. After all, if the Constitution is truly mysterious, if it speaks in tongues and riddles, then the layperson must seek the guidance of the high priests to discern its meaning. And who are the high priests of constitutional interpretation if not the justices of the Supreme Court?

But we have no reason to ascribe such motives to Justice Stevens, whose mild-mannered approach to his judicial role seems entirely genuine. So it seems worth asking whether the Constitution is indeed "mysterious" in some genuine sense. One kind of mystery about the Constitution is explored in Michael Kammen's excellent work of social history, *A Machine That Would Go of Itself.* Kammen notes that, although the Framers of the Constitution intended that it be accessible to the people, throughout most of our nation's history the Constitution has been revered more as a sacred object to be worshipped than as a text to be read and interpreted.[2]

Indeed, even as we complete this book, current events are providing a striking example of the paradox Kammen identifies. We have in mind the controversy surrounding President Bush's proposed constitutional amendment to permit the federal and state governments to impose criminal sanctions upon those who "des-

I

ecrate" the American flag. The proposal is a response to the 1989 and 1990 Supreme Court rulings, which we applaud, that flag-burning is a form of political expression protected by the First Amendment.[3]

One might think that opponents of the amendment would point to the ways in which a constitution revised to include such a provision would be inferior to our current Constitution. For example, it is not at all obvious why, out of all the forms of constitutionally protected political expression that a local or national majority might find offensive—including political rallies by Nazis, pornography depicting women as dominated objects, and racist language, to name just a few—only flag burning should be punishable. In addition, there would be real practical difficulties in fairly enforcing a flag desecration statute. What would happen to someone who burned a picture of a flag, or a flag with forty-nine stars?

Such arguments have been made in the press and elsewhere. However, because it is widely perceived as political suicide to avow open support for governmental toleration of flag-burning, in the House of Representatives the amendment was defeated primarily because of a different argument: that we shouldn't tamper with the Bill of Rights. As Representative David Skaggs of Colorado put it, "[w]hat assurance is there that this excision in the Bill of Rights, once breached [sic], would not lead to others?"[4] By relying upon the perceived inviolability of the Bill of Rights, opponents of the proposed amendment have turned to the one political icon strong enough to match the flag in its symbolic appeal, the mysterious Constitution.

In this book we focus on one source of the mystery surrounding the Constitution: how is it that different readers of the Constitution draw such very different conclusions about its commands? The importance of such disagreement is enormous. For example, on one day in June 1990, the Supreme Court decided two cases dealing with abortion[5] and one about the right to die.[6] Two of those cases were decided by a margin of one vote. Indeed, 37 of the 129 cases heard by the Supreme Court in 1990 produced five-to-four splits.[7] When matters so fundamental as life and death turn on one unelected justice's interpretation of a mysterious document, it is worth unraveling the mystery.

Another way to put the question is to ask: What does it mean to *read* this Constitution? What is it that we do when we *interpret* it? Why is there so much controversy over *how* it should be interpreted—and why is so much of that controversy, these days in particular, not limited to the academy or to the profession, but so public that it makes the evening news and the front pages?

The controversy reached its most feverish pitch during the 1987 hearings on the nomination of Judge Robert H. Bork to serve as a Supreme Court justice. Although Judge Bork's record was distorted by some who opposed his nomination,[8] the Senate's decision to withhold its consent was based in large part on its rejection of Judge Bork's belief that a quest for the "original intent" of the Framers of the Constitution is the only proper method of interpreting the Constitution.[9] The claim that the Framers' intent should control our contemporary reading of the Constitution is one of the subjects we address in this book.

The furor over the Supreme Court's flag-burning decisions and the controversy over the Bork nomination are, of course, only the most recent examples of widespread disagreement over how the Constitution ought to be read. The Supreme Court's school prayer decisions in the 1960s, its abortion decision in 1973, and its reaffirmation of those controversial decisions in the mid-1980s gave many critics ample incentive to criticize the Court's interpretation of the Constitution.[10] So too have the Supreme Court's more recent rulings narrowing the previously recognized abortion right and questioning the constitutionality of some affirmative action plans provided fuel for other critics.[11] Indeed, such criticism of the Court has been the rule rather than the exception throughout most of this century. Disagreement with the Supreme Court's laissez-faire rulings of the early twentieth century, and the Court's invalidation of key New Deal measures into the 1930s, provided ample motive for people to attack the Court during those years.[12] Similarly, disagreement with the desegregation and the reapportionment decisions decades later spurred loud reactions against the jurisprudence of the Warren Court.[13] But the *level* and *tone* of the public debate reached something of a new pitch by the end of the 1980s—one that has not been heard at this intensity in so sustained a way since FDR's assault on the "Nine Old Men" in the presidential election of 1936.

We intend here to take the dispute seriously—not to regard it simply as a mask for disagreement with the Court's results on particular issues, or as a mere excuse to oppose one or another judicial nominee, although to some extent it *is* simply a matter of whose ox has most recently been gored. Recognizing that such substantive disagreement plays a large role in bringing critics out into the open, in other words, does not justify inattention to the content of that disagreement. Proceeding from the premise that there is a real dispute over ways of interpreting the Constitution, we shall try to understand what the structure of that dispute is.

One of our main purposes here is to demystify the process of reading the Constitution. No doubt in part because it is easier to destroy than to create, easier to deconstruct than to construct, we begin in Chapter 1 by looking at some ways *not* to read that document. In Chapter 2 we ask if what we know about what the Constitution is *not* can tell us anything about what it *is*. We conclude that it can, and sketch a method for those whose offices require them to read the Constitution to protect fundamental liberties.

In Chapter 3 we explore the source of disagreement in so many cases of modern constitutional law, what we call the "levels of generality" problem. The problem is this: virtually any form of behavior, when described in sufficiently general terms, will qualify as part of the "liberty" protected by the Constitution and the Supreme Court's earlier cases. How then are justices to choose a level of generality without merely imposing their own values? Before proposing our partial answer to this vexing question, in Chapter 4 we pause to look outside the law and ask what is so special about reading the *Constitution*. How is it different from reading a novel? And how is writing a legal opinion different from constructing a mathematical proof?

Finally, we turn in Chapter 5 to a 1989 suggestion by Justice Scalia that he has solved the levels of generality problem. We analyze his proposed solution and conclude that it is inadequate. We then offer our own modest proposal for constraining, though not eliminating, judicial value choice in the elaboration of constitutional liberties.

The reader who expects to find in these pages a decoding device that will solve all constitutional puzzles will be disappointed. For our goal is to demystify not by prescribing any orthodox interpretation, but by suggesting what we hope will be fruitful questions.

I

—————

How Not to Read the
Constitution

FROM ITS VERY CREATION, the Constitution was perceived as a document that sought to strike a delicate balance between, on the one hand, governmental power to accomplish the great ends of civil society and, on the other, individual liberty. As James Madison put it in *The Federalist Papers,* "[i]f men were angels, no government would be necessary. If angels were to govern men, neither external nor internal controls on government would be necessary. In framing a government which is to be administered by men over men, the great difficulty lies in this: you must first enable the government to control the governed; and in the next place oblige it to control itself. A dependence on the people is, no doubt, the primary control on the government; but experience has taught mankind the necessity of auxiliary precautions."[1] Although Madison initially opposed the inclusion of a Bill of Rights in the Constitution, as his correspondence with Thomas Jefferson shows, he became convinced that judicially enforceable rights are among the necessary "auxiliary precautions" against tyranny.[2]

In the Constitution of the United States, men like Madison bequeathed to subsequent generations a framework for balancing liberty against power. However, it is only a framework; it is not a blueprint. Its Eighth Amendment prohibits the infliction of "cruel and unusual punishment," but gives no examples of permissible or impermissible punishments. Article IV requires that "[t]he United States shall guarantee to every State in this Union a Republican Form of Government," but attempts no definition of republican government. The Fourteenth Amendment proscribes state abridgments of the "privileges or immunities of citizens of the United States," but contains no catalogue of privileges or immunities.

How then ought we to go about the task of finding concrete commandments in the Constitution's majestically vague admonitions? If there is genuine controversy over how the Constitution should be read, certainly it cannot be because the disputants have access to different bodies of information. After all, they all have exactly the same text in front of them, and that text has exactly one history, however complex, however multifaceted. But of course different people believe different things about how that history bears on the enterprise of constitutional interpretation.

Thomas Grey of Stanford, in a wonderful essay entitled "The Constitution as Scripture," builds on some earlier work by Sanford Levinson of Texas, Robert Burt of Yale, and the late Robert Cover of Yale.[3] Grey asks provocatively whether some regard the history of the Constitution, both prior to its adoption and immediately thereafter, and even the history subsequent to that, as somehow a *part* of the Constitution—in much the same way that some theologians consider tradition, sacrament, and authoritative pronouncements to be part of the Bible. And he asks whether perhaps others regard the history, and certainly the post-adoption tradition and the long line of precedent, as standing entirely apart from the Constitution, shedding light on what it means but not becoming *part* of that meaning—in much the way that other theologians consider the words of the Bible to be the sole authoritative source of revelation, equally accessible to all who read it, in no need of the intervention of specialized interpreters and thus not to be mediated by any priestly class. What role *ought* history to play?

Perhaps the disputants agree on what *counts* as "the Constitution," but simply approach the same body of textual and historical materials with different visions, different premises, and different convictions. But *that* assumption raises an obvious question: How are those visions, premises, and convictions relevant to how this brief text ought to be read? Is reading the text just a *pre*text for expressing the reader's vision in the august, almost holy terms of constitutional law? Is the Constitution simply a mirror in which one sees what one wants to see?

The character of contemporary debate might appear to suggest as much. Liberals characteristically accuse conservatives of reading into the Constitution their desires to preserve wealth and privilege, and the prevailing distribution of both. Conservatives characteristically accuse liberals of reading into the Constitution *their* desires to redistribute wealth, to equalize the circumstances of the races and the sexes, to exclude religion from the public realm, and to protect personal privacy. How are we to understand such charges and countercharges?

Back to the Founding

It might help to begin at the beginning. One astute observer of language and law, James White of the University of Michigan English Department and the Michigan Law School, has noticed an important difference between the Declaration of Independence and the Constitution.[4] The Declaration, he points out, is a proclamation by thirteen sovereign states at a moment of crisis. It is a hopeful cry. It is an attempt to justify revolution. It is addressed to the King of England, and even more significantly to the conscience of Europe. It is a call for assistance and support.

The Constitution makes a stark contrast. It is neither a justification nor a plea. It is a proclamation issued in the name of "We the People of the United States." Its preamble declares a bold purpose: "to form a more perfect Union, establish Justice, insure domestic Tranquility, provide for the common defence, promote the general Welfare, and secure the Blessings of Liberty to ourselves and our posterity." It then proceeds to "ordain and establish this Constitution for the United States of America" by setting forth a distribution of powers and by declaring various limits on those powers.

That seems a supremely confident and courageous act—to create a nation through words: words that address no foreign prince or distant power, but the very entity called into being by the words themselves; words that address the government that they purport to constitute; words that speak to subsequent generations of citizens who will give life to that government in the years to come.

The idea that words can somehow infuse a government with

structure, and impose limits on that structure—that language can directly power the ship of state and chart its course—has played an important role in what Americans, particularly in our early years but to some extent even today, have tended to think about the Constitution. As James Russell Lowell wrote in 1888, "[a]fter our Constitution got fairly into working order it really seemed as if we had invented *a machine that would go of itself.*"[5]

Justice Oliver Wendell Holmes drew on a similar image, but had no similar illusions, when he chose his words in 1920 in the case of *Missouri v. Holland.*[6] He wrote:

> when we are dealing with words that also are a constituent act, like the Constitution of the United States, we must realize that they have called into life a being the development of which could not have been foreseen completely by the most gifted of its be-getters. It was enough for them to . . . hope that they had created an *organism;* it has taken a century and has cost their successors much sweat and blood to prove that they created a *nation.*[7]

"The case before us," Holmes went on, "must be considered in the light of our whole experience and not merely in that of what was said a hundred years ago. . . . We must consider what the country has become in deciding" what the Constitution means.[8] Holmes had no doubt that the very *meaning* of the thing we call "the Constitution"—even though its words, as marks on parchment carefully preserved at the National Archives, remain unaltered—was a reality partly reconstructed by each generation of readers. And he had no doubt that that was as the Framers of the Constitution themselves originally intended. They were, after all, *framing* the Constitution, not painting its details. Why else call them the "Framers"?

How different an image that is from the originalist image suggested by Gary Wills in his book *Inventing America.*[9] Wills writes that to understand the true meaning of a text, we must forget what we have learned from the events that transpired between the text's creation and the present. Even taking Wills's vision on its own terms, there is every reason to see a paradox in it, because many of those who wrote the text of the original Constitution or voted to approve it, or wrote or voted to approve some of its amendments, supposed that the meaning, at least of the more general terms being deployed, was inherently variable. They supposed that the examples likely to occur to them at the time of the creation would not be forever fixed into the meaning of the text itself. Thus, even supposing that what the Framers thought about the Constitution should be the touchstone of constitutional interpretation, it need not be the case that the Constitution's broad language would have to be interpreted in such a way that it speaks only to issues that already existed two hundred years ago.

Another proponent of locating the ultimate interpretive authority in the Framers' intent, Raoul Berger, has argued that the original intent of the Framers is "as good as written into the text" of the Constitution.[10] That viewpoint became something of a manifesto for former Attorney General Meese, who often spoke and wrote of a "jurisprudence of original intent."[11] But consider the practical difficulties of applying such a theory when, for example, Berger looks at the Fourteenth Amendment, a text proposed to the states by Congress and voted on by no fewer than thirty-seven state legislatures.[12] Berger purports to know that the original purpose of the Fourteenth Amendment was far less noble than some of us have come to believe; the primary intended beneficiaries of the Fourteenth Amendment, he tries to show, were racist white Republicans.[13] And therefore, he says, giving the Fourteenth Amendment the meaning that the Supreme Court has given it in modern times is ahistorical and illegitimate.

Let us suppose that Berger's history is correct—that one really could make that confident an assertion about something as fleeting and elusive as collective intent. In fact, suppose that the *real* purpose of those who wrote the Fourteenth Amendment was to *deny* equality to the freed slaves to whatever degree would prove politically possible. That is, suppose the Fourteenth Amendment was a palliative designed to preserve peace, but that the reason for not writing so racist a credo into the Constitution's *text* was a sense that some of the Amendment's support might not withstand such candor.

Even if this supposition were historically correct, and even if you believed that original intent should control constitutional interpretation, it still does not follow that it would be legitimate to read the Fourteenth Amendment to effect the hidden racist agenda. Why not? For one reason, because the Fourteenth Amendment became "part of th[e] Constitution" in accord with Article V—the provision of the Constitution that describes how amendments become law. They become law when they are ratified through a specified process by a certain number of states. There is nothing in Article V about ratifying the secret, hidden, and unenacted intentions, specific wishes, or concrete expectations of a group of people who may have been involved in the process of enacting a constitutional guarantee.

Constitutional commentators sometimes seem to forget that history serves to illuminate the text, but that only the text itself is law. Consider, for example, the Second Amendment, which reads: "A well regulated Militia, being necessary to the security of a free State, the right of the people to keep and bear Arms, shall not be infringed." Unique among the provisions of the Constitution, the Second Amendment comes with its own mini-preamble, setting forth its purpose: to foster a "well regulated Militia." This purpose has little to do with individuals possessing weapons to be used against their neighbors; as a result, the Second Amendment has not been interpreted by the courts to prohibit regulation of private gun ownership.[14] Nonetheless, in an essay provocatively titled "The Embarrassing Second Amendment," Sanford Levinson of the University of Texas argues that because the enactment of the Second Amendment took place during an era that valued armed citizens as a civic republican bulwark against tyranny, it must be interpreted according to civic republican traditions.[15] Levinson may well be right that the Second Amendment was enacted against a civic republican background that saw individual gun-ownership as part of the "right of the people to keep and bear Arms" that promotes a "well regulated Militia." But the Second Amendment did not enact the background understanding. The only purpose it *enacted* is the one contained in its text, for only its words are law. And in modern circumstances, those words most plausibly may be read to preserve a power of the state militias against abolition by the federal government, not the asserted right of individuals to possess all manner of lethal weapons.

Thus, the constitutional text itself seems to preclude an interpretive method that relies too heavily upon history alone. But even if the originalist paradigm were not internally inconsistent, there would be good reason to question its basic assumptions. Dean Paul Brest of Stanford, in an article called "The Misconceived Quest for the Original Understanding," suggests that once we take into account the elaborate evolution of constitutional doctrine and precedent, we cannot avoid seeing the original document and its history recede as a smaller and smaller object into a distant past.[16] He says it is "rather like having a remote ancestor who came over on the Mayflower."[17] Of course, Brest is offering only a description of the way things are. Even if the description is accurate, some might say it is not a very good *prescription* of the way things *ought* to be. Perhaps the Court, and commentators, should return more often to the Mayflower and pay somewhat less attention to all the accumulated barnacles. But as with the sailing ship, this Mayflower is venerated less because of the vessel it was than because of the voyage it began. Return to the source, and we find an invitation not to linger too obsessively in the past.

Consider, for example, those of the Framers' generation who thought that the very common practice of disqualifying the clergy from public office was consistent with the Constitution. They included Thomas Jefferson, who thought that the clergy ought to be excluded from legislatures. Yet mightn't the very Framers who believed the practice to be constitutional in their day nonetheless have been surprised by a suggestion that clergy disqualification therefore could *never* be declared unconstitutional? In fact, some of the Framers, along with Jefferson, later concluded that the clergy could not validly be excluded. And when the Supreme Court finally held in a case from Tennessee in the late 1970s that disqualifying clergymen from public office is indeed unconstitutional, Justice Brennan was entirely correct to observe in his concurring opinion that "[t]he fact that responsible statesmen of the day, including some of the . . . Constitution's Framers, were attracted by the concept of clergy disqualification . . . does not provide historical support for concluding that those provisions are harmonious with the Establishment Clause."[18]

Or consider again those who voted to propose the Fourteenth Amendment to the states, or voted to ratify it. There is very little doubt that most of them assumed that segregated public schools were, at the time, entirely consistent with the Fourteenth Amendment. And yet would any of them have said, if pressed, that the Fourteenth Amendment could *never* be invoked, as events unfolded, to reach a different conclusion about segregated public schooling? Who among us can doubt that the Supreme Court was entirely correct when in 1954 it finally held that it could not turn the clock back to 1868, that it had to consider what public education had *become*—to examine its status "in light of its full development and its present place in American life"—in order to decide whether segregation could still be deemed constitutional?[19]

It is not that the *meaning* of the Fourteenth Amendment had changed. From its enactment the Equal Protection Clause was understood to render unconstitutional the subjugation of an entire race with the force of law. It took us longer than it should have to concede that segregating people in the public schools *amounted* to subjugating an entire race by force of law. But the basic principle remained constant.[20] It is quite likely that many of the original Framers and those responsible for enacting subsequent amendments, although perhaps not all, would have been rightfully horrified at Wills's prescription of amnesia as part of the proper method of applying their words to a changing reality.

Reading the Constitution or Writing One?

The belief that we must look beyond the specific views of the Framers to apply the Constitution to contemporary problems is not necessarily a "liberal" position. Indeed, not even the most "conservative" justices today believe in a jurisprudence of original intent that looks only to the Framers' unenacted views about particular institutions or practices. Consider the following statement made by a Supreme Court justice in 1976:

> The framers of the Constitution wisely spoke in general language and left to succeeding generations the task of applying that language to the unceasingly changing environment in which they would live. . . . Where the framers . . . used general language, they [gave] latitude to those who would later interpret the instrument to make that language applicable to cases that the framers might not have foreseen.[21]

The author was not Justice William Brennan or Justice Thurgood Marshall, but then-Justice William Rehnquist. Or consider the statement by Justice White, joined by Justice Rehnquist in a 1986 opinion for the Court: "As [our] prior cases clearly show, . . . this Court does not subscribe to the simplistic view that constitutional interpretation can possibly be limited to the 'plain meaning' of the Constitution's text or to the subjective intention of the Framers. The Constitution," wrote Justice White, "is not a deed setting forth the precise metes and bounds of its subject matter; rather, it is a document announcing fundamental principles in value-laden terms that leave ample scope for the exercise of normative judgment by those charged with interpreting and applying it."[22]

So the "conservatives" on the Court, no less than the "liberals," talk as though *reading* the Constitution requires much more than passively discovering a fixed meaning planted there generations ago. Those who wrote the document, and those who voted to ratify it, were undoubtedly projecting their wishes into an indefinite future. If writing is wish-*projection,* is reading merely an exercise in wish-*fulfillment*—not fulfillment of the wishes of the *authors,* who couldn't have begun to foresee the way things would unfold, but fulfillment of the wishes of *readers,* who perhaps use the language of the Constitution simply as a mirror to dress up their own political or moral preferences in the hallowed language of our most fundamental document? Justice Joseph Story feared that that might happen when he wrote in 1845: "How easily men satisfy themselves that the Constitution is exactly what they wish it to be."[23]

To the extent that this is so, it is indefensible. The authority of the Constitution, its claim to obedience and the force that we permit it to exercise in our law and over our lives, would lose all legitimacy if it really were only a mirror for the readers' ideas and ideals. Just as the original intent of the Framers—even if it could be captured in the laboratory, bottled, and carefully inspected under a microscope—will not yield a satisfactory determinate interpretation of the Constitution, so too at the other end of the spectrum we must also reject as completely unsatisfactory the idea of an empty, or an infinitely malleable, Constitution. We must find principles of interpretation that can anchor the Constitution in some more secure, determinate, and external reality. But that is no small task.

One basic problem is that the text itself leaves so much room for the imagination. Simply consider the preamble, which speaks of furthering such concepts as "Justice" and the "Blessings of Liberty." It is not hard, in terms of concepts that fluid and that plastic, to make a linguistically plausible argument in support of more than a few surely incorrect conclusions. Perhaps a rule could be imposed that it is improper to refer to the preamble in constitutional argument on the theory that it is only an introduction, a preface, and not part of the Constitution *as enacted*. But even if one were to invent such a rule, which has no apparent grounding in the Constitution itself, it is hardly news that the remainder of the document is filled with lively language about "liberty," "due process of law," "unreasonable searches and seizures," and so forth—words that, although not *infinitely* malleable, are capable of supporting meanings at opposite ends of virtually any legal, political, or ideological spectrum.

It is therefore not surprising that readers on both the right and left of the American political center have invoked the Constitution as authority for strikingly divergent conclusions about the legitimacy of existing institutions and practices, and that neither wing has found it difficult to cite chapter and verse in support of its "reading" of our fundamental law. As is true of other areas of law, the materials of constitutional law require construction, leave room for argument over meaning, and tempt the reader to import his or her vision of the just society into the meaning of the materials being considered.

In the book *Constitutional Choices,* one of us argued that as a result of this fluidity, judges have to acknowledge, as they read the Constitution, that they cannot avoid making at least *some* basic choices in giving it content.[24] For Judge Richard Posner, who reviewed the book, that idea was heresy. In his view, the moment we openly avow the need for choice, it follows that we argue "in effect . . . that the Constitution is exactly what we want it to be."[25] Never mind that on other occasions Judge Posner has not been quite so hostile toward interpretation. In a 1987 magazine article, for instance, he denounced "strict constructionis[m]," noting that "[t]here has never been a time," and demonstrating that, for reasons of pragmatics and policy, there "could [not be a time,] . . . when the courts of the United States, state or federal" could merely "find and apply" the law.[26] The essence of Judge Posner's particular complaint in his book review is the suspicion that we liberals want the Constitution to be "the charter of a radically egalitarian society."[27]

What, then, is Judge Posner to make of the fact that the sort of Constitution an egalitarian would want, the sort that he or she would probably set out to write if given that responsibility, differs in significant respects from the Constitution that we actually have—a Constitution that no doubt was written in significant part to protect the propertied minority from those with less wealth? What other meaning can one *possibly* give to the contract and property clauses of the Constitution? Conversely, what are we to make of the fact that Judge Posner seems to read in the Constitution as it exists a sweeping ban on race-specific affirmative action, even though the text says absolutely nothing, and, so far as we can determine, the history does not support, requiring government to be color-blind when it seeks to eradicate historic discrimination?[28] Are we to suppose that Judge Posner's Constitution is what *he* wants it to be?

Any reader of the Constitution as it is should be able to imagine numerous ways in which it differs from her ideal constitution, as she would wish it to be. If *we* were writing a Constitution for the United States, we might well favor a constitutional provision guaranteeing decent housing and employment for every person. We might even favor a constitutional provision setting a ceiling on the intergenerational transmission of wealth. And, of course, we would certainly disagree with each other about the merits of various other proposed provisions. But, having read and reread the document as it exists, and having thought hard about it, we both agree that it is quite impossible to read *our* Constitution as including either of those two provisions. Indeed, one's sense that in the ideal society a constitution would include this or that provision ought to make each reader of the Constitution skeptical about the argument that such provisions can be teased out of the current language, in order to avoid falling into the trap of believing, as Justice Story put it, that "the Constitution is exactly what [each reader] would wish it to be."[29]

In this sense, although we agree with much of what Ronald Dworkin has written in his powerful book, *Law's Empire,* the breadth of his notion of interpretation seems troubling. In his view, to "interpret" a cultural or social practice, or a legal text, is to make of it the best thing of its kind that one believes it is capable of being. As Dworkin would have it, for example, the interpreter of a play or a poem seeks to understand it in such a way that it becomes the best play or the best poem that it can be. And so he urges that the interpreter of a constitutional concept like "due process of law" or "equal protection of the laws" should seek to understand that concept in accord with the interpreter's larger vision of what a good constitution should be like.[30] This approach is certainly not excluded in any *a priori* way by the meaning of the concept of "interpretation"; work in interpretive theory, or hermeneutics, suggests that the concept is indeed broad enough to take in what writers like Dworkin have in mind, and we argue in Chapter 4 that Dworkin's view of interpretation can generate useful insights for constitutional law.

Nevertheless, the enterprise that we are or should be about when we advance an argument in the Constitution's name must be more bounded than Dworkin's enterprise. The moment you adopt a perspective as open as Dworkin's, the line between what you think the Constitution *says* and what you wish it *would* say becomes so tenuous that it is extraordinarily difficult, try as you might, to maintain that line at all. How can one maintain the line—given the ambiguity of the Constitution's text, the plasticity of its terms, the indeterminacy of its history, and the possibility of making noises in the Constitution's language that *sound* like an argument for just about anything? What does it mean to suggest that the Constitution imposes serious constraints on choice? How can one maintain, in other words, a stance in which reading the Constitution differs from writing one?

One thing that is plain is that there would be no real difference between those two enterprises if what we meant by "the Constitution" included not only the text and the history and tradition of its interpretation but also something as vague and ineffable as the essence of the American spirit—what Thomas Grey has described as the "grand and cloudy Constitution that stands in our minds for the ideal America, earth's last best hope, the city on the hill."[31] *That* Constitution, which seems to be the one that commentators like Michael Perry of Northwestern occasionally evoke even when they purport to be discussing something more modest, may be the stuff of Bicentennial celebrations, but it is difficult to think of it as binding law—law that unelected judges should be entrusted to expound in an enforceable way.[32]

One of us (Laurence Tribe) is evidently regarded by some as an admirer of that gauzy sort of Constitution, figuring as one of the chief villains in such derisive works as Henry Monaghan's essay, "Our Perfect Constitution"—accused by Monaghan of always seeing a silver lining even in the gray and sometimes bleak language of the document.[33] Whether or not there was ever any basis for Monaghan's characterization, we do not espouse anything quite as mystical as all that here. While the Constitution may be, as Justice Stevens has described it, "[m]ysterious,"[34] it is not mystical—and not even lost in the mists of the ideal.

Surely close attention to history will prevent us from deploying the Constitution as a kind of crystal ball in which we might see whatever we wish to see. Yet however helpful history may be—and although it is indefensible to ignore it—history alone cannot serve to domesticate, discipline, and bind down text. History alone cannot eliminate the possibility of constructing out of the Constitution's phrases at least a *theoretical* argument for nearly any desired conclusion.

Nonetheless, such a theoretical argument would not necessarily be an argument that would deserve to be taken seriously, much less an argument that could fairly persuade. It may not be possible to "prove," in the way one proves a mathematical conjecture to be true or false, that a particular fanciful, ingenious argument about the Constitution simply doesn't count as a plausible interpretation. But from the impossibility of that sort of proof, all that follows is that law, like literature, is not mathematics—as we spell out more precisely in Chapter 4. It should not be terribly surprising to learn that judicial deliberation, like all legal discussion, cannot be reduced to scientific processes of deduction and induction, although some people apparently continue to be surprised by this truism.

The impossibility of airtight "proof" does not, however, translate—as some seem to believe it does—into such total indeterminacy that *all* interpretations of the Constitution are equally acceptable. Nor does it follow that the only way to judge an interpretation is to ask whether it advances or retards your vision of the good society. It is possible to do much better than that, although not nearly as well as some might wish.

Part of the difficulty is in no sense peculiar to law, but relates, rather, to the deep and abiding problem of how to imagine, conceptualize, and understand the process and the practice of giving reasons, of engaging in rational persuasion, without leaning on notions of timeless, universal, and unquestionable truth. A great many people have lost faith in the idea of the timeless, the universal, and the unquestionable. Yet somehow, in their ordinary lives, they can still distinguish what sounds like a good argument from what sounds like sophistry: they *know* that slavery and murder are wrong, even if they cannot derive these truths from first principles. Nor does it require treating judges or other interpreters of the Constitution as if they had access to some mathematical algorithm of interpretation to conclude that for practical reasons it makes sense to entrust to people removed from the political fray the process of reason-giving, even in an environment where we lack the metric—the external measure— to prove conclusively that reason X is no good while reason Y is decisive. A number of philosophers, most notably Hilary Putnam, have made extremely useful contributions to our understanding of what it means to give reasons in a world unbolstered by ultimate truth.[35] But the processes of constitutional interpretation and adjudication obviously cannot be called off while that enterprise is being pursued, especially if you believe that that enterprise will likely go on forever.

Two Interpretive Fallacies

In the meantime, we can focus our interpretive energy on concrete features of the Constitution that we actually have. In beginning to sort out good and bad ways of arguing about what *this* Constitution means, we can make considerable headway by inquiring what it is about some modes of discourse, some modes of conversation that are put forth as "constitutional argument," that makes them suspect from the start. What is it about some purported modes of constitutional analysis that makes them implausible candidates for ways of reading the Constitution we actually have?

In effect, we want to offer some negative observations about ways *not* to read the Constitution, before turning in the remaining chapters to the more affirmative project of *reading* the Constitution, against the backdrop of several actual as well as hypothetical cases. We have already rejected originalism as one way not to read the Constitution. Two additional ways not to read the Constitution are readily apparent; we will call them reading by *dis*-integration and reading by *hyper*-integration.

When we say reading by "dis-integration," we mean approaching the Constitution in ways that ignore the salient fact that its parts are linked into a whole—that it is *a Constitution,* and not merely an unconnected bunch of separate clauses and provisions with separate histories, that must be interpreted. When we say reading by "hyper-integration," we mean approaching the Constitution in ways that ignore the no less important fact that the whole contains distinct parts—parts that were, in some instances, added at widely separated points in American history; parts that were favored and opposed by greatly disparate groups; parts that reflect quite distinct, and often radically incompatible, premises. In the beginning, the Constitution as proposed by Congress in 1787 was ratified by the requisite number of states in 1787 and 1788. Twenty-six amendments were added, ten of them in 1791, the remainder from 1795 to 1971—and so became "valid," under Article V, "to all intents and purposes, as part of this Constitution." In addition, other watershed events in American history, such as the Supreme Court's 1937 "switch in time" upholding New Deal legislation that had previously been deemed unconstitutional, have been viewed by some as informal amendments of the Constitution.[36] The Constitution of the United States is thus simultaneously a single entity or structure *and* a collection of enactments by the people; the whole is not a unitary, seamless proclamation. These observations may seem too obvious to be worth making. Nonetheless, they serve to disqualify much of what passes as constitutional argument and interpretation. Those who try to see in this complicated collage of compromise over time one single vision, and who then proceed to argue from that vision, have lost sight of the constraints imposed by our experience under a written constitution. They are not reading the Constitution we have, but a hyper-integrated constitution for which they yearn.

Dis-Integration

Consider more closely, then, the first fallacy—that of dis-integration. Let us begin with a straightforward example, one that was a favorite of former Chief Justice Burger. The Fifth Amendment says that "no person . . . shall be deprived of life, liberty, or property, without due process of law." Chief Justice Burger used to argue, as have others, that the authors of that language obviously must have contemplated that, *with* "due process of law," a person *may* be deprived of life. Therefore, the argument goes, capital punishment is constitutional. It's very simple; why should the Court struggle over it?

The conclusion may or may not be right. Whether the death penalty is unconstitutional in an era when the overwhelming majority of industrialized nations have rejected it is a perplexing question. But Chief Justice Burger's proposed method of answering it is profoundly dis-integrated and is not really a way of interpreting *this* Constitution, because the Fifth Amendment is only part of the document. There is also the Eighth Amendment, ratified as a separate part of the Constitution. It says that "cruel and unusual punishments" shall not be imposed. Is the death penalty, then, cruel and unusual? Quite clearly, it was not considered cruel and unusual in 1791, when both the Fifth Amendment and the Eighth Amendment were ratified. But it might be so today, as Justice Brennan has argued.[37] The fact that another constitutional clause evidently contemplates that death might be inflicted by government without offense to *that* part of the Constitution doesn't answer the question. Indeed, if the Fifth Amendment *did* answer it, we would be left with another dilemma, since it also seems to sanction hacking off people's limbs—by its command that no person shall be "twice put in jeopardy of life or limb." Yet no one would seriously argue today that bodily mutilation, employed on occasion as a punishment during colonial times, could withstand scrutiny under the Eighth Amendment.

Again, it seems to be that what the Fifth Amendment suggests as an answer becomes only a question once the Eighth Amendment is consulted.

Consider another example. It has been urged by some, including Mark Tushnet of Georgetown, that we ought to read the Constitution as requiring socialism—as obliterating the institution of private property. How else, he asks, can we make sense of the ideal of equality that underlies the constitutional mandate of the equal protection of the laws?[38] If *all* the Constitution contained were an equal protection clause, perhaps something might be said for that view. But the view becomes untenable if we also remember that, in various of its parts, the Constitution expressly affirms, sanctifies, and protects the institution of private property. It says that neither the state nor the federal government may deprive anyone of property without "due process of law," and that "private property [shall not] be taken for public use without just compensation."[39] Indeed, many state constitutions around the time of the Revolution, perhaps reflecting a view that all property ultimately belongs to the state as custodian for the people as a whole, included no such clause. Its inclusion in the *federal* constitution marked a significant rejection of the model of "state as ultimate owner."[40] It is a dis-integrated "reading" of the Constitution to lift one provision out, hold it up to the light, and give it its broadest possible interpretation, while ignoring the fact that it is immersed in a larger whole.

Consider one final example of dis-integration. From time to time, the Supreme Court has invoked the Tenth Amendment as a basis for saying that some powers that are delegated to the Congress by the Constitution, such as the power to tax or the power to spend, nonetheless violate the reserved rights of the states. Justice Brennan and a number of others on the Court have replied that this is a linguistic impossibility, because the Tenth Amendment states that all "powers *not* delegated to the United States by the Constitution, nor prohibited by it to the States, are reserved to the States respectively, or to the people." It appears to follow that, if a power *is* "delegated to the United States"— delegated to Congress by Article I in the field of interstate commerce, for example—then the power in question *can't* be reserved to the states. Thus, the states have *no* reserved rights, no matter how big the federal government becomes, no matter how sweeping its powers come to be.[41]

If the Tenth Amendment stood alone, Justice Brennan's argument would have considerable force. But think about the Tenth Amendment embedded in a Constitution that includes other provisions as well. What did the Framers know to be true about the Constitution when they wrote the Tenth Amendment the way they did, expressly reserving to the states only those powers with respect to which the national legislature was *not* delegated authority by the Constitution? One of the things they knew was that the national legislature was structured so as to represent, directly, the institutional interests of the states—since, at the time the Tenth Amendment was added to the Constitution, the United States Senate was composed of two senators from each state "chosen by the Legislature thereof."[42] It was not until the Seventeenth Amendment was ratified in 1913 that senators were "elected by the people" directly.

Thus, part of what the Tenth Amendment's structure presupposed was altered in 1913. That alteration in turn seems relevant to how the entire question of the reserved rights of the states should be considered in the latter part of the twentieth century. If the states can no longer directly represent their institutional interests in the Senate, perhaps there is room to reexamine the premises underlying the pre-1913 understanding of the Tenth Amendment. The Supreme Court hinted that this consideration is at least *relevant* when in 1985 Justice Brennan's view of the Tenth Amendment finally prevailed.[43] Whether it is *dispositive* raises complex questions of interpretive method to which we will return in Chapter 2. For, to make sense of the Tenth Amendment, in addition to considering the effect of the Seventeenth Amendment we must focus on a great deal more. The basic point here, however, is that whatever our overarching theories about knowledge and interpretation might be, we can make real progress in reading the Constitution by eliminating at the start arguments that are not eligible for treatment as constitutional interpretation because they entail reading not *this* Constitution, but a desiccated, dis-integrated version of it.

Hyper-Integration

At the other extreme there stands the fallacy of *hyper*-integration—of treating the Constitution as a kind of seamless web, a "brooding omnipresence" that speaks to us with a single, simple, sacred voice expressing a unitary vision of an ideal political society. Of course, that would have been an impossible view to maintain early in our history: the fugitive slave clause, the Constitution's prohibition on any interference by Congress with the slave trade until the year 1808, the apportionment formula for the House of Representatives, which regarded a slave as equal to three-fifths of a person, and the other accommodations to the institution of slavery that were written into the text would have been difficult to square with many of the ideals found elsewhere in the document.[44]

But it would be a fundamental mistake to suppose that, after ratification of the Civil War amendments, all such basic contradictions were eliminated from the Constitution, which suddenly became a coherent, consistent document. Conflicting visions—of liberal individualism on the one hand and civic republicanism on the other; of national supremacy as opposed to states' rights; of positivism as opposed to natural law—pervade the Constitution throughout its many parts. The notion that the Constitution embodies an immanent, unitary, changeless set of underlying values or principles—whether procedural or substantive or structural—seems an extraordinary intellectual conceit, one inconsistent with the character of the Constitution's various provisions as concrete political enactments that represent historically contingent, and not always wholly coherent, compromises in a document that was made in stages, incrementally, over a period of two centuries.

This is not to say that we share the view expressed by Bruce Ackerman of Yale, who proposed in his Storrs Lectures that we have *several* "Constitutions," some of them essentially unwritten but reflected in such national crises and readjustments as the Great Depression and the New Deal.[45] To be sure, the Constitution viewed as a historically evolving set of principles and premises has undergone crucial discontinuities at several such junctures. Yet surely there nonetheless remains but one Constitution of the United States. That Constitution cannot be confused with the unitary expression of a single idea—whether that idea be a grand Newtonian design of checks and balances, a great Darwinian vision of moral evolution, a Burkean construct for the perpetuation of tradition, a scheme for the perfection of representative democracy, or any of the large number of other ideals to which commentators over the years have sought to subordinate the considerably less tidy Constitution *as it actually exists*. We would go further: the undeniably plural and internally divided nature of the Constitution is not a sad reality; it may well be among the Constitution's greatest strengths.

It seems to have become a professional habit of constitutional commentators to superimpose their own preferred vision of what the Constitution is "really" meant to do, and then to sweep aside all aspects of its text, history, and structure that do not quite fit the preferred grand design. That is not constitutional interpretation as we would wish to practice it, though every reader of the Constitution may at times come close to reducing the Constitution to some central unity, the better to derive corollaries from whatever core vision she believes it embodies. In one essay published several years ago, one of us even went so far as to propose that, but for the manifest institutional unacceptability of its doing so, the Supreme Court might, in theory, hold a constitutional amendment incompatible with the grand design of the Constitution—the norms and premises pervading the document as a whole.[46] Although the article never suggested that the Court could properly strike down a duly ratified amendment (it stated the opposite), it came quite close to the view that had been advanced by Walter Murphy of Princeton—that the Constitution, correctly understood, expresses a vision sufficiently coherent that amendments radically incompatible with that vision are not law.[47]

Consider, for example, the task that would confront the Supreme Court if, in order to reverse the Court's 1989 and 1990 flag-burning decisions, the Constitution were amended to enable the federal and state governments to impose criminal sanctions on someone who "knowingly mutilates, defaces, physically defiles, burns, maintains on the floor or ground, or tramples upon any flag of the United States." That was the language of the federal statute properly struck down in *United States v. Eichman*.[48] Presumably, the terms of any flag desecration amendment that might ever be ratified would not disturb the First Amendment per se. It would be an amendment *in addition to* the First Amendment: both would be part of the amended Constitution.

Suppose that after ratification of the flag desecration *amendment,* Congress were to reenact the flag desecration *statute* struck down in *Eichman.* Would it then be obviously constitutional? In the 1989 flag-burning case, the Supreme Court noted that protection for "expression of dissatisfaction with the policies of this country [is] situated at the core of our First Amendment values."[49] The statute would strike at the "core" of the First Amendment, since it is difficult to imagine that someone who burns an American flag expresses anything but "dissatisfaction with the policies of this country." Given the importance of the First Amendment to our constitutional scheme of individual liberty and self-government, might this entitle the justices to rule that since the First Amendment is still part of the Constitution it trumps the flag desecration amendment, and to hold therefore that flag-burning is still protected speech, notwithstanding the flag desecration amendment? Such a hyper-integrationist position would, in our view, be illegitimate. To be sure, there may be no adequate political *theory* that can reconcile wide-ranging freedom of expression generally with an explicit exception for the United States flag; yet the need for doctrinal consistency does not empower the Supreme Court to ignore the text or the undeniable purpose of a duly enacted amendment. Difficult as the task might be, the Supreme Court would have to go about drawing lines between protected expression on the one hand, and unprotected flag-defilement on the other.

The sort of view that would allow the Supreme Court to invalidate a duly enacted amendment is a clear symptom of *not* interpreting the Constitution; little could better illustrate the hyper-integrationist fallacy. To attribute any unitary mission to the Constitution "as a whole" is to cross the line between *reading* the document and *writing* one of your own.

John Hart Ely, former dean of Stanford Law School, in an elegant and brilliant but in at least one way deeply flawed work, *Democracy and Distrust,* may have crossed that line when he proposed reading the entire document as having the central, nonsubstantive aim of perfecting democracy by reinforcing the effective workings of representative government.[50] From that perspective, there turn out to be some especially problematic clauses in the Constitution. There is one clause in particular that sounds awfully substantive, saying that no state "shall abridge the privileges or immunities of citizens of the United States."[51] And there is the Ninth Amendment, about which we will have much to say in Chapters 2 and 5. Ely does *not* say that the text of these clauses, or their history, shows them to be concerned only with representative government. He says, rather, that—since the general point of the Constitution as a whole is to preserve representative government, and since judicial activism is most readily defended when it reinforces rather than undermines representation—we ought to squeeze those clauses into that vision.

But reading things *out* of the Constitution in order to bring the document into line with a theory seems no more defensible than reading things *into* the Constitution for the same reason. To paraphrase Ely's remarks made in another context, a representation-reinforcing, democracy-perfecting form of judicial review—one that finds judges crusading *only* to make representative government work better and *never* to protect substantive human rights independent of representative government—may be "a thing of beauty and a joy forever," but if it is not part of the Constitution, we have no business proclaiming it in the Constitution's name.[52]

Dean Jesse Choper of Berkeley seems to us to be guilty of much the same fallacy when he powerfully develops the position that judicial review should be excluded altogether in matters of federalism and the separation of powers, primarily so that the federal judiciary in general, and the Supreme Court in particular, can conserve its resources for the cases that Choper believes really require active judicial involvement—cases in which the Court must protect despised minorities and unpopular claims of human rights—inasmuch as the separate branches of the national government, and the states, are capable of taking care of their own interests without such judicial help.[53] This sort of political analysis seems unpersuasive even on its own terms: would the people inclined to protest the Court's protection of some downtrodden group be much appeased if the Court were to remove itself scrupulously from disputes about the separation of powers and federal-state relations? The idea that the Court could husband its resources in that way seems rather naive.

But even if we accepted Choper's premises, we could not accept his conclusion. Constitutional protection for one branch of the federal government against another—the sort of thing we saw in the Supreme Court's legislative veto decision of 1983,[54] and in its Gramm-Rudman decision of 1986[55]—or constitutional protection for state sovereignty, which we consider in greater detail in Chapter 2, cannot properly be subtracted from the text on the instrumental or consequentialist ground that the Supreme Court believes, however plausibly, that its resources are better spent elsewhere. Whatever else it may be, the Constitution certainly is *not* a charter for maximizing the influence of the federal judiciary in defense of liberal or, for that matter, conservative causes. Any mode of "interpretation" that distorts constitutional parts in support of any such whole is really not a mode of interpretation at all.

Neither the political left nor the political right has any monopoly on these unitary visions of the constitutional enterprise. One of the most extraordinary examples in recent decades is found in a book called *Takings,* by Richard Epstein of the University of Chicago.[56] Epstein makes an extremely clever but stunningly reductionist argument that the whole Constitution is really designed to protect private property. Thomas Grey has aptly dubbed this "the Malthusian Constitution."[57] It is a constitution in whose name Epstein would evidently be prepared to strike down progressive taxes, the Social Security system, minimum wage laws, and, indeed, *all* laws that "general economic theory" condemns as tending to reduce overall wealth.[58] Can a constitution reflecting as diverse an array of visions and aspirations as ours really be reducible to such a sadly single-minded vision as that?

Indeed, even if that vision were an elevated and lofty one, the idea that the whole Constitution could be harnessed to it seems wrong. David Richards of New York University, in a book entitled *Toleration and the Constitution,* works mightily to advance a constitutional vision in which the many provisions of the document expressing respect for personal dignity and individual diversity are woven into a unified fabric.[59] His ultimate ambition is to "take seriously the larger historical meaning of a written constitution as an expression of a coherent political theory."[60] But the Constitution, in our view, could not possibly express "a coherent political theory," however sympathetic and humane we might find its substance. It seems almost a contradiction in terms to suppose that one could read a constitution composed as ours has been as though it were an expression of any unified philosophy.

A healthy suspicion of hyper-integration has significance beyond the negative. Instead of simply serving to *disqualify* otherwise attractive candidates for methods of constitutional interpretation, the insight might also provide something of an answer to those who would attack particular approaches to interpretation as subject to internal contradictions and anomalies. Many critical legal scholars, for example, have developed elaborate and often very insightful analyses designed ultimately to show that what they call "liberal constitutional scholarship" cannot meet various demands of coherence—that it will contain internal contradictions.[61]

It has been a commonplace in constitutional commentary for a long time to deride various approaches as insufficiently democratic or insufficiently majoritarian in character and, therefore, as contradicting some supposed need of the Constitution *as a whole* to affirm democracy.[62] But where is that "need" of the Constitution "as a whole"? After all, every right protected by the Constitution is a right protected *against* majority legislation. It would certainly be illegitimate for a hyper-integrationist majoritarian to declare that individual liberties are unenforceable because they are anti-majoritarian. Of course, what follows from the recognition that our system of government limits what democratic majorities may do is not the proposition that judges may freely substitute their values for those produced by the electoral process. As one of us has noted, someone who adhered to Nobel laureate Kenneth Arrow's social choice theory—which holds that there is no way to combine individual preferences to produce one "true" preference of the whole society—might presume that courts, rather than elected legislators or executives, are in the best position to determine what is right for society.[63] But that observation about the consequences of one theory of how government actually works should not be confused (as some apparently have confused it[64]) with a prescription for how judges interpreting our Constitution ought to act. For despite its specific prohibitions on certain majority actions, at the very least the Constitution establishes a strong presumption in favor of leaving most policy choices to democratic majorities in the absence of some applicable prohibition. The Constitution, although not democratic "as a whole," is largely democratic.

When all of the Constitution's supposed unities are exposed to scrutiny, criticisms of its inconsistency with various readers' sweeping visions of what it ought to be become considerably less impressive. Not all need be reducible to a single theme. Inconsistency—even inconsistency with democracy—is hardly earth-shattering. Listen to Walt Whitman: "Do I contradict myself? Very well then, I contradict myself." "I am large, I contain multitudes," the Constitution replies.[65]

2

Structuring Constitutional Conversations

ALTHOUGH IT IS VERY USEFUL to know how *not* to read the Constitution, ultimately, judges, legislators, and executive officials charged with interpreting the Constitution must be able *to* read it. Reading the Constitution does not require an overarching theory of constitutional interpretation. That would be hyper-integration. But just as we strive to avoid the Scylla of hyperintegration, so too must we steer clear of the Charybdis of disintegration. Although we cannot give a completely consistent *theory* of constitutional interpretation, we can at least sketch some acceptable *approaches* to the enterprise. If the task we have set for ourselves sounds halting and tentative, it is because the questions to which constitutional interpretation are addressed are so basic and so difficult. More often than not, we have no answers, and those we offer are almost never held with certitude. We do not attempt to offer the last word on the Constitution's meaning; when a last word is possible the Constitution will have lost its relevance to an ever-changing society. Less ambitiously, but perhaps more realistically, we hope to contribute to a useful dialogue on reading the Constitution, a "constitutional conversation."[1]

Lessons from the Constitution's First Two Centuries

It is only natural during this period of the constitutional bicentennial that many people, throughout our country and around the world, have been taking an unusually close look at the sorts of answers our system has given, and continues to give, to questions of constitutional interpretation. In some countries those questions tend to be submerged because no judicially enforceable written constitution exists to be interpreted and applied. In England, for example, it is still true, as a British court put it with striking modernity nearly three centuries ago, that "[a]n Act of Parliament can do no wrong, though it may do several things that look pretty odd."[2]

But an ever larger number of nations in the post–World War II period have chosen our more rebellious path rather than England's traditional one. More nations would do so, William Van Alstyne of Duke has suggested, if they could somehow be assured that judges would not be too ingenious in their reading of constitutional texts.[3] His notion is that, witnessing the controversy over what our courts have done with the relatively brief text of our Constitution, others may find it best simply to say: "No thank you, we would rather avoid all of that." But the lesson of our first two centuries under a written constitution, we would argue, is really quite different from the lesson Van Alstyne suggests some in other countries might perceive. Our history indicates, rather, that judicial ingenuity, along with statesmanship of many other sorts, has probably been indispensable to our success as a constitutional democracy. After all, the lines of precedent that most of us deeply regret—including decisions like the infamous *Dred Scott* opinion, which held that blacks were not capable of being citizens of the United States and gratuitously announced the unconstitutionality of the Missouri Compromise, thereby helping to provoke the Civil War—followed at least as often from overly mechanical, wooden, or insensitive interpretations as from overly creative and ingenious ones.[4] Yet a further lesson is that there exists no formula that could eliminate altogether the need for judicial choice, although there are certainly formulas that try to *hide* that need behind proclamations of "original intent" or of the "clear meaning" of the text. Finally, the American experience teaches that the best way to achieve wisdom in constitutional interpretation is to subject all constitutional arguments and decisions to constant analysis and continuing critique, both in terms of the text and in terms of our traditions for construing it.

For the Constitution, despite Lowell's vivid description in 1888, is *not* entirely "a machine that would go of itself."[5] Fundamentally, the Constitution is, rather, a text to be interpreted and reinterpreted in an unending search for understanding. A central theme of our argument in Chapter 1 was the need to recognize that this search cannot be rendered perfect and infallible by any agreed-upon definition of a unitary goal, or by any single mode of proceeding. Indeed, we closed by celebrating our Constitution's multiplicity—its character as a text containing distinct but not always consistent subtexts. We praised the Constitution's resistance to reductionist analyses designed to squeeze it into any single philosophy of state or of society.

To be able to chart a course between the equally hazardous shores of dis-integration and hyper-integration, we must know how the Constitution's text *channels* choice without *eliminating* it. Before turning to what all might agree are "difficult" cases, it will be useful to consider some "easy" ones. We will see that the Constitution's channeling function is fully present even when we are applying the most seemingly specific of constitutional clauses. For it is a fundamental mistake to suppose that weighty problems of interpretation arise only in the hardest cases—only where the issue is one about which the text is unusually vague or unusually ambiguous. That is a favorite gambit of certain Supreme Court commentators, who point to a division among justices on an issue and say: "Look how they disagree, five to four. It must be that they're not really reading the Constitution, but just seeing in it a mirror of what they want to believe." Therefore, let us consider briefly, before turning to more involved illustrations, a couple of examples in which the text is quite clear—as clear as these things get, at any rate—and in which disagreement is nonetheless unavoidable.

Simple Clauses Don't Necessarily Make Easy Cases

Consider the clause of Article I of the Constitution that reads: "No Bill of Attainder or ex post facto Law shall be passed."[6] Now "Bill of Attainder" is a term of art. The prohibition is widely understood to mean that legislatures may not single out those whom they wish to punish. After President Nixon left office under well-known circumstances, Congress passed a statute identifying Richard Milhous Nixon *by name* and providing that, unlike other ex-presidents, he could not have access to his White House papers and tapes until they had been fully catalogued and reviewed by the General Services Administration. Congress was evidently unwilling to generalize its rule to cover any future president who might resign during impeachment proceedings.

A divided United States Supreme Court nonetheless concluded that this Act of Congress was not a Bill of Attainder.[7] The Court reasoned that Mr. Nixon was not being punished, even though this was a somewhat humiliating restriction—one to which no past president had ever been subjected, and one which, by its terms, could apply to no future president. Besides that, the majority of the Court held, Richard Nixon is "a legitimate class of one."[8] Several dissenters took the position that this law is a forbidden Bill of Attainder: it imposes a stigmatizing disability on someone driven from power, whether justly or not, in a way that explicitly identifies the individual or individuals to be so penalized.[9]

Did the justices disagree because some of them wanted to punish Nixon while others wanted to spare him? Were they merely reading their personal or political views into the Bill of Attainder Clause? This hardly seems plausible, since anyone who knows the specific justices and how they voted would probably conclude that some justices on each side of the *Nixon* case would have preferred to read the Constitution the way the other side in fact read it. They were not voting their political preferences, or even their general ideology, but were voting on the basis of conscientiously different readings of what the Bill of Attainder Clause proscribes. Conscientious readers of the Constitution may differ in their understanding in a case like this, involving even a fairly narrow and precise constitutional provision.

If the Bill of Attainder example shows that the justices do not merely vote according to their narrow political or personal preferences, perhaps they adhere to more general "conservative" or "liberal" interpretive philosophies. Although it is certainly the case that no justice is without such tendencies, the range of cases that arise under the Constitution, and the judgments for which they call, defy any such simple hyper-integrated classification. To see this, let us examine another phrase that is at least relatively specific, compared with some of the grand and cloudy clauses with which we sometimes deal in constitutional law: the First Amendment's prohibition against "any law abridg[ing] the freedom of speech or of the press."

Consider the following real case. A state statute of New York authorized the closure of any building determined to be a public health nuisance, upon the finding that the building was being used as a place for "prostitution" or "lewdness." The Village Books and News Store, an adult bookstore in Kenmore, New York, owned by Cloud Books, Inc., sold sexually explicit, but not legally obscene, books and magazines. A deputy sheriff observed patrons of the store engaging in sex acts on the premises within plain view of the proprietor. Prostitutes were also seen soliciting business there. The store was found at trial to be a "public health nuisance" under the statute. Pursuant to the statute, the premises were ordered closed for a year.

As one might imagine, the owners appealed. Everyone involved agreed that the books and magazines being sold on the premises were "speech," entitled to First Amendment protection. The issue was whether closing the bookstore for a year under these circumstances amounted to a forbidden "abridgment" of speech. Specifically, did the state have to meet the standard, which is imposed in First Amendment cases, of showing that its legitimate objectives required something as drastic as closing this store down for a whole year? In other words, did the state have to prove that a less restrictive remedy would have been inadequate to abate such nuisances? Was this a gratuitously wide-ranging suppression of speech?

The highest court of New York State ruled that closing the bookstore down in this way was indeed a violation of the federal constitutional right to free speech. That court held the First Amendment applicable, required the state to meet a least restrictive remedy test, and found that the test was not met.[10] In its view, the legitimate purposes of the State of New York could be served by something less drastic than closure of the bookstore for an entire year. And, in fact, the state court was able to invoke the original intent of the First Amendment's Framers in partial support of its view. Original intent arguably did support the result, since a central purpose of the First Amendment was to prevent the government from imposing prior restraints on publication—

and an order closing a bookstore or a movie theater obviously restrains a publishing activity in advance.

When the case reached the United States Supreme Court, three justices agreed with that view.[11] The other six justices saw the case differently. To them, it was merely incidental that this happened to be a bookstore. After all, the statute itself had nothing to do with speech. Its use against this business was triggered not by the *books* being sold, but by the *sex* being peddled. The case is *Arcara v. Cloud Books, Inc.;* one reason it is less widely known than it ought to be is that the opinion was handed down on the same day the Supreme Court struck down the Gramm-Rudman Balanced Budget Act, which attracted all the media attention that day.[12]

Regardless of whether one generally takes a broad or a narrow view of the First Amendment, former Chief Justice Burger's majority opinion in the *Arcara* case is very persuasive. If the First Amendment requires New York State to show that a one-year closure is the least restrictive alternative simply because a bookstore was involved, then consider what follows. Suppose, for example, that a television anchorman like Tom Brokaw or Dan Rather, to avoid being late for the evening news broadcast, decides to drive at eighty miles per hour or run ten red lights in a row. When a state trooper arrests him and sends him to jail for the night, the anchorman could say, "But you're suppressing speech! You have to prove that jail is necessary. How about just a fine?" The First Amendment would become involved whenever the enforcement of otherwise valid and neutral laws happens incidentally to restrict speech. Surely Justice O'Connor—whose *Arcara* concurrence inspired the newscaster example—is correct that this cannot be a sound, sensible reading of the First Amendment.[13]

Justice O'Connor's concurrence, which Justice Stevens joined, was quite sensitive: she agreed that the state court had applied too stringent a standard to the challenged New York actions, but quite properly left open the possibility of a First Amendment claim if a city were to use a nuisance statute like this as a *pretext* for closing down a bookstore because of the books it sold.[14] There was nothing in the record of this case suggesting that that had been done.

Justices Brennan, Marshall, and Blackmun dissented. In their view, whether or not the law was used as a pretext, it was applied unconstitutionally. There had been no showing that the amount of suppression of speech that resulted from the bookstore closure was necessary to achieve the legitimate aims of New York. "Until today," they wrote, "this Court has never suggested that a State may suppress speech as much as it likes, without justification, so long as it does so through generally applicable regulations" unrelated to expressive conduct.[15] The dissenters made a respectable argument, but, in our view, they and the state court were wrong.

How do we account for the fact that First Amendment liberals (like the authors) could disagree with the "liberal" justices concerning the correct result in *Arcara?* Certainly it is not because we are more personally offended than those three justices were by the sexual activity on the premises in that case. Are we less concerned than they are about the value of free speech? Is it that we are strict constructionists while they are loose constructionists? Are we—along with the "conservatives" on the Court—less concerned with original intent? After all, the state court invoked "original intent." None of these explanations seems right.

Like the case involving Richard Nixon, *Arcara* nicely illustrates how honest and conscientious readers of a quite specific constitutional provision, engaged in the process of genuine interpretation, can reach entirely opposite conclusions, regardless of their overall philosophical leanings. The existence of room for disagreement, in other words, is not proof that what is going on does not deserve to be called interpretation—that we are watching some kind of shell game—any more than the existence of differences in the interpretation of any text suggests that something other than interpretation is really afoot.

We cannot improve upon Justice Kennedy's description of how an honest effort to read the Constitution can result in the reader's feeling bound to an interpretation that he or she does not like. In the 1989 flag-burning case of *Texas v. Johnson,* Reagan appointees Antonin Scalia and Anthony Kennedy joined Justices Brennan, Marshall, and Blackmun to strike down a conviction under Texas's flag-burning statute. Justice Kennedy wrote a separate concurrence in which he noted:

> The hard fact is that sometimes we must make decisions we do not like. We make them because they are right, right in the sense that the law and the Constitution, as we see them, compel the result. And so great is our commitment to the process that, except in the rare case, we do not pause to express distaste for the result, perhaps for fear of undermining a valued principle that dictates the decision.[16]

If there can be nonideological disagreement about the meaning of even a fairly precise text, disagreement seems even more inevitable in those situations where the text itself is famously imprecise, where it may not even be clear which *part* of the constitutional text applies. In the remainder of this chapter we shall focus on language of this kind. What can we do with situations in which the constitutional nostrils flair—where there is a sense that there may be something wrong, but one reads through the document and can't quite pin down where that sense comes from?

A Troubling Question of Federalism

To illustrate such a situation, consider the following hypothetical case. Assume that Congress passes the Home-Rule Act of 1991, abolishing home rule in all the states that now have it, and centralizing state and local governance in the state capitals—telling the states, in other words, that they cannot delegate a common kind of blank-check lawmaking authority to their cities and counties, towns and municipalities. Analysis of such a case must examine the various reasons Congress might have for doing such a thing. But quite apart from the reasons, one must ask, in thinking about possible challenges to the validity of a federal statute that cuts this deeply into the way state and local governments decide to structure themselves, whether the statute seems to offend any relevant text in the Constitution.

Many people would gravitate toward the Tenth Amendment. It reads: "The powers not delegated to the United States by the Constitution, nor prohibited by it to the States, are reserved to the States respectively, or to the people." Perhaps the very first question that a constitutional interpreter would ask is whether the Home-Rule Act of 1991 might be invalid under the Tenth Amendment on the ground that it attempts to exercise a power "not delegated to the United States by the Constitution."

To answer that question one would have to ask what power Congress might be exercising here. Most likely, it is exercising the commerce power of Article I—Congress's power "[t]o regulate Commerce . . . among the several States."[17] To someone in 1920, that might not have seemed so obvious, but in the period from 1937 to the present most readers have found in the Commerce Clause an extraordinarily broad authority for Congress to regulate virtually everything, however local, that might have any impact on interstate commerce.[18] And obviously, the exercise of power by localities pursuant to home rule provisions might have such an impact.

Indeed, there are some important Supreme Court decisions upholding application of the Sherman Antitrust Act to the actions of cities and towns. Boulder, Colorado, for example, acting under the Colorado home rule provisions, restricted competition among cable franchises. The Supreme Court held that, when Boulder did that, its actions were subject to the Sherman Act.[19] The actions of Colorado itself are exempt from the Act; the Supreme Court in 1943 interpreted the Act as not reaching action by the sovereign states.[20] But in the *Boulder* case the Supreme Court held that, when municipalities exercise power pursuant to home rule provisions, they do not inherit the state's immunity from the Sherman Act. They are left out in the cold.

A sequel to *Boulder* arose in Berkeley, California, in a case in which property owners argued that Berkeley's rent control ordinance was a violation of the Sherman Act, because it too was passed pursuant to a home rule provision. Therefore, they claimed that Berkeley did not step into California's shoes—that it did not inherit California's immunity from the antitrust laws. In representing the City of Berkeley in the Supreme Court, one of us (Laurence Tribe) argued that the justices did not have to reach the immunity issue because, in fact, municipal rent control simply does not violate the antitrust laws, even though a private rent-fixing cartel would. The Court, by an 8–1 vote, agreed.[21]

But the Commerce Clause would certainly have *allowed* Congress to reach such municipal action had it so chosen. And, as the *Boulder* case illustrates, the Commerce Clause apparently allows

Congress to regulate the way in which the states relate to their municipalities. For if the state itself had *mandated* an anticompetitive stance by Boulder, that municipal action would have been immune from all challenge under the Sherman Act. It is only because the state chose to let Boulder roll on its own, as it were, that the immunity evaporated.

But where under the Commerce Clause does Congress get the power to regulate the relationship between a state and its municipalities? How might the very *existence* of home rule have an impact on interstate commerce? Here one must perhaps be a bit imaginative, but the Court has done that to sustain all kinds of laws that do not appear to be much concerned with commerce as such. For example, Title II of the Civil Rights Act of 1964, which prohibits racial discrimination in public accommodations, was upheld by the Supreme Court not as an exercise of Congress's power to enforce the Equal Protection Clause of the Fourteenth Amendment—as the lay observer may have reasonably expected—but as a valid exercise of Congress's power to regulate interstate commerce.[22] So the Commerce Clause really is quite broad.

Congress, for example, might decide that unfettered, autonomous home rule cities are less likely to take the national economic interest into account than are cities that are kept on a short leash by the state legislature. And, being less likely to take the national interest into account—more likely therefore to act parochially—such home rule jurisdictions are more likely, cumulatively, to pose a threat to the smooth flow of interstate commerce.

The Court has upheld, as falling within the reach of Congress's commerce power, actions founded on rationales no more tenable than that. But notice that, even though it is clear that Congress is indeed acting pursuant to a power expressly delegated by the Constitution, it is still cutting deeply into the very *structure* of state government. The question one might then want to ask is this: Does the Constitution somehow reserve to the states any residual sphere of autonomy—a core of fundamental sovereignty—or must we conclude, simply because Congress is exercising a nationally delegated power, that there is no room left to make a states' rights argument? The structure of the Tenth Amendment may appear to indicate that there *is* no room left.

Recall our discussion of the Tenth Amendment in Chapter 1. We noted that its language seems to create a binary, either/or system: the powers *not* delegated to the United States are reserved to the states. Either a power is delegated to the United States, or it's not. If it is delegated, it cannot be reserved. End of argument.

Well, not quite. For one thing, the text does not say that *only* the powers not delegated are reserved. And, in any event, with another provision, sitting right next to the Tenth Amendment, the Court has not been stopped cold by the text. In construing the Eleventh Amendment, the Court has indeed *ignored* part of the text. By its terms, the Eleventh Amendment excludes from the general federal judicial power lawsuits that are brought against a state without its consent in federal court "by Citizens of another State." But the Supreme Court has had no trouble amending that language over the years to read, in effect, "by Citizens of another State *or* of the same State."[23] Indeed, the garden-variety use of the Eleventh Amendment is to prevent a citizen of State A from suing State A in a federal district court.

That the Court has occasionally rewritten the Constitution, however, doesn't make such a practice right. Many commentators, including one of us, have severely criticized the Court's recasting of the Eleventh Amendment.[24] But by comparison, a reading of the *Tenth* Amendment to bar congressional interference with home rule provisions would appear to be a far more radical judicial usurpation. After all, it is one thing to *expand* an amendment a little—to say that its purposes require grafting something on; it is quite another to rewrite it so as to change its structure. The apparently binary structure, if not the literal text, of the Tenth Amendment would go out the window if the Court were to hold that, under that amendment, there can be powers delegated to the federal government and *nonetheless* reserved to the states.

Of course one might say, as we indicated in Chapter 1, that the Tenth Amendment does not sit in majestic solitude in the Constitution. Things have changed since it was written in 1791. Congress's powers have expanded radically. And the Seventeenth Amendment in 1913 stripped the states of their direct representation in the Senate, replacing legislative appointment of senators with direct election of senators. As we have argued, given such changes, there might be room to reexamine the meaning of the Tenth Amendment. But however much one reexamines the amendment, it still appears to create a binary structure. Revising a specific constitutional provision that radically, on the ground that the surrounding circumstances have changed, really *does* expose the Court to the charge that it is not interpreting the Constitution, but rewriting it.[25]

How about going outside of the Constitution's text? That is what the Supreme Court did in 1976 to articulate a sphere of state sovereignty protected from federal legislative incursions, in *National League of Cities v. Usery*.[26] There, the Court did not really rely on the Tenth Amendment; the amendment was mentioned only as an illustration.[27] Instead, by a five-to-four margin, the Court relied on the general structure of the Constitution and its presupposition of state sovereignty. It did that in order to hold that Congress, by exercising its affirmative powers under the Commerce Clause to extend minimum wage, maximum hour, and overtime protection to state and municipal employees, violated state sovereignty. That was the holding of *National League of Cities*. But the doctrine lasted less than a decade.

National League of Cities was overturned in 1985 in the *Garcia* decision,[28] but not because the Court was embarrassed at having ignored the Tenth Amendment, or at having rewritten it. Rather, Justice Blackmun reversed his vote to form a new five-to-four majority largely for the quite pragmatic reasons that, for ten years, the Court had not proved capable of drawing very well the lines called for by *National League of Cities,* and that, as a political matter, states probably didn't *need* the Court's help: they could fight it out for themselves through their elected representatives. Justice Powell, in a powerful dissent, strongly criticized that approach. He asked in effect: Would you liberals, who make that argument in this case, say that individual rights don't need this Court's protection because *individuals* are, after all, represented in the legislature? If you take rights seriously, they are rights *against* the majority. They cannot be forgotten simply because, as a practical political matter, those who hold them might also have a lot of political clout.[29]

The decision overruling *National League of Cities* was not very persuasive, as we have just suggested. But then *National League of Cities* itself was problematic. It is difficult to imagine how an approach to constitutional interpretation that is not in any way connected with the text qualifies as *reading* as opposed to *writing* the Constitution.

How about relying on the whole structure of the Constitution—not the Tenth Amendment considered alone, but the entire structure? That approach was most powerfully advanced in Charles Black's 1969 book, *Structure and Relationship in Constitutional Law.*[30] He essentially urged that meaning should be found not only in the four corners of the document but, as it were, in the angles and shapes of its joints and seams—reading not only the lines of the text but between the lines, focusing as closely on how the pieces fit together as on their individual shapes.

One would not suppose that so-called strict constructionists would find that notion very appealing. But the justices who *have* found it appealing include Justice—now Chief Justice—Rehnquist, Justice Powell, Justice O'Connor, and former Chief Justice Burger. In *Nevada v. Hall,*[31] the Court faced the question whether states should be immune from suits brought against them by citizens of sister states suing in their own state, not federal, courts. The majority of the Court found no such constitutional immunity, holding that the Constitution confers no protection against such suits in state court. In dissent, then-Justice Rehnquist took the position that such protection was implicit in the very *structure* of the Constitution. He argued that "[t]he tacit postulates [of the constitutional plan] are as much engrained in the fabric of the document as its express provisions."[32]

Surely this reliance on the "tacit postulates" of the whole plan is incompatible with "strict constructionism." Was not Justice Rehnquist guilty of the hyper-integrationist fallacy—of purporting to find in the Constitution one seamless system of tacit postulates, not subject to any requirement that such postulates be anchored in any particular constitutional text?

But if Justice Rehnquist's technique of seeing the tacit postulates afloat in the heavens above, or seeing them swim in the melted core beneath the Constitution, seems a bit too "loose constructionist"—and if trying to anchor the tacit postulates to the text of the Tenth Amendment won't quite do because that text must be mangled in order to achieve the goal—does it follow that we must give up? In our hypothetical case, do states possess the power to decide on home rule only at the whim of Congress?

If, as we suggested in Chapter 1, the Constitution is a kingdom of many mansions, each replete with numerous chambers, then, to paraphrase the post-structuralist, we might ask: "Is there another text in the room, one that might be relevant and helpful?"[33] Perhaps there is. When Justice O'Connor dissented, for example, from part of the Supreme Court's 1982 decision in *Federal Energy Regulatory Commission v. Mississippi,* a case in which Congress had told the public utility regulatory commissions of the states how to structure their agendas, she wrote that "federalism enhances the opportunity of all citizens to participate in representative government."[34] And she quoted de Tocqueville: "'[T]he love and the habits of republican government in the United States were engendered in the townships and in the provincial assemblies.'"[35] She spoke of the republican spirit, meaning not "Republican" with a capital "R" but civic republicanism—the public-spiritedness of community.

Consider then Article IV, Section 4, of the Constitution, an explicit text: "The United States shall guarantee to every State in this Union a Republican Form of Government." How about *that* provision as our text for protection of states' rights? There are two major obstacles. The first is that the Supreme Court held long ago that the Republican Form Clause does not create judicially enforceable rights for individuals. An individual cannot go into court and say, "The government of my state is not representative enough. I want it restructured."[36] But there are two answers to that. First, the Court has allowed individuals to go into court and make that very argument under the Equal Protection Clause of the Fourteenth Amendment in the reapportionment decisions, extended in 1986 to cases of political gerrymandering, in *Davis v. Bandemer.*[37] The logic of these cases would appear to cast doubt on the continuing vitality of the Supreme Court's older reading of the Republican Form Clause. Second, even if it is still true that the Republican Form Clause does not guarantee enforceable rights to *individuals,* it does not follow that it fails to guarantee enforceable rights to *states.* After all, it says that "[t]he United States *shall* guarantee *to every State* in this Union a Republican Form of Government." There is a powerful argument that the clause should be enforceable in an otherwise proper suit by a state against the federal government.[38]

The second point to be made is that home rule is not itself required by the Republican Form Clause. Many states do not have home rule; surely we cannot say that *they* have given up representative government. One quite plausible answer is that, although home rule itself is not required by the Constitution's guarantee of a republican form of government, the ability to *choose* between home rule and centralization arguably *is* so required. The authority to decide, consistent with such provisions as the Equal Protection Clause of the Fourteenth Amendment, how a state's people will represent themselves and participate in their own governance—how their system of government will be structured—is the essence of self-government and is protected, or should be deemed protected, by the Republican Form Clause.[39]

From this example we can draw four lessons about reading the Constitution: (1) relying on an amendment written so that it cannot plausibly be made to apply won't do; and (2) relying on an overall, unstructured system of tacit postulates is too loose; but (3) searching the Constitution for other applicable texts is always an available option, so long as we are careful (4) to require that the text upon which we settle is able to support the weight that we would make it bear.

Looking for Unenumerated Rights

Let us try to apply these lessons to another hypothetical law. Suppose a municipality has enacted a local ordinance requiring all families to eat at home at least once each month, with only family members present, and to precede that meal with a "moment of thankful silence." Is there any text in the Constitution that might be invoked to challenge such an ordinance?

Of course one could turn to the Establishment Clause of the First Amendment. This "moment of thankful silence" looks suspiciously like prayer; for the government to command such a moment seems to entail government endorsement of religion. In *Wallace v. Jaffree*[40] the Supreme Court struck down, as a forbidden establishment of religion, an Alabama statute that did not even *require* a moment of silence but simply *permitted* teachers to schedule such a moment of silence "for meditation or voluntary prayer" at the start of each public school day. Nobody was required to pray, and no teacher was required to set aside the moment.

Nonetheless, the Supreme Court held that this statute violated the Establishment Clause as applied to the states through the Fourteenth Amendment. The Court's majority stressed two features of the statute absent in the imaginary case that we have posited. The Court stressed that, in its debate over the statute, and in the statute's text, the Alabama legislature had explicitly referred to prayer in a manner obviously designed to endorse that religious practice. The Court also stressed that the issue arose in the context of the public schools—so that the power of government, which forced students to attend, was harnessed by religion, and so that a governmental institution, the public school, *borrowed* part of its authority from sacred symbols, in a dubious mix of church and state.

In his dissent, then-Justice Rehnquist pointed out that the wall of separation between church and state is more a judicially created metaphor than anything to be found in the text of the Constitution.[41] (Notice how readily the "tacit-postulate" justice becomes a strict constructionist, perhaps implying that Justice Rehnquist would have approved of our conclusion in Chapter 1 that some methodological inconsistency in constitutional interpretation is unavoidable.) The early presidents, he stressed, proclaimed Thanksgiving; despite that holiday's religious significance, there was no suggestion that they were violating the Establishment Clause. And, he indicated, there is no evidence that the Framers would have objected even to voluntary *prayer* in public schools. Yet, as he noted, this was not even prayer—just a moment of silence for meditation *or* prayer.

Justice O'Connor, concurring with the majority, offered a powerful rejoinder to Justice Rehnquist.[42] She argued that this history was inconclusive: public schools barely existed when the First Amendment was written; they were not a powerful presence even when the Fourteenth Amendment was written and ratified. We might recall the observation from Chief Justice Rehnquist, noted in Chapter 1, that we must apply the Framers' basic concepts to unforeseen circumstances.[43] If one takes that reminder seriously, then Justice O'Connor seems to have the better of the argument. Indeed, even if the historical evidence did show that in an earlier era religion and government mixed with each other to a greater extent than they do now, it is difficult to see why that should settle the matter. As Justice O'Connor observed in a 1989 case involving religious displays on public property, "no one acquires a vested or protected right in violation of the Constitution by long use, even when that span of time covers our entire national existence and indeed predates it."[44]

But what follows for our hypothetical case? In this case, no public school is involved; there is no reference to prayer; it is only an expression of thanks that the law says must be given before the evening meal. Here the historical record is ambiguous: Madison's Thanksgiving proclamations don't prove much since, after his presidency was over, he argued that, on reflection, even those Thanksgiving proclamations had improperly mingled government and religion.[45] And requiring Thanksgiving proclamations monthly by families could well be deemed a violation of the Establishment Clause.

But this isn't an official proclamation. The law merely requires the family to give thanks in its own way, and it doesn't require them to give thanks to anyone in particular; it simply says there should be a "moment of thankful silence." The law doesn't involve the *government* doing anything; it only tells the *family* what to do. And, in a sense, that cuts against the Establishment Clause argument. But, although government is not officially proclaiming religion through the ordinance, a different kind of argument becomes apparent—an argument about intrusion into the freedom of the family, perhaps its free exercise of religion.

Moreover, an argument could be made that the law violates the right to free speech. After all, the law by its terms prohibits speech: it compels silence. Of course, a supporter of the law might respond that the law does not single out any particular message, and that it really is a very minimal intrusion: it commands silence for only one "moment" per month. Viewed in this light, the arguably substantial government interest in fostering family togetherness could be seen to outweigh the small burden on speech.[46]

However, it doesn't really make sense to view the burden that the law places upon speech as a sort of side effect of some speech-neutral policy. True, one effect of the government's telling families to be silent is that during the time they are silent they cannot speak their minds. But more than that, the silence itself is pregnant with meaning. The law requires "thankful silence." It requires families to express thanks, and in that way to "speak," through their silence. Yet the First Amendment's protection for freedom of speech includes the right not to speak. That is the lesson of the case of *Wooley v. Maynard,* in which the Supreme Court ruled that New Hampshire could not compel its citizens to display the motto "Live Free or Die" on their automobile license plates.[47] So it is a delicious irony of our hypothetical mealtime regulation that governmentally compelled silence violates the right not to speak.

Leaving these First Amendment questions aside, let us focus on a different aspect of this case by extracting religion and speech from the picture altogether. Let's delete the requirement of a moment of thankful silence. Let's have a simpler law: once a month, at least, every family must sit down and have dinner together—just the family members, no friends. They don't have to say anything; they can just sit there and munch. Conversely, they don't have to be silent. But they *must* eat together as a family at least once a month. The maxim underlying such a requirement might be something like "a family that chows together grows together."

How are we to analyze such a law? In the early 1970s the Supreme Court confronted a case not entirely unlike this one—a case involving food stamps. Congress had passed an amendment to the food-stamp statute providing that, if a family invites non-members to live with the family, it loses its food stamps, even though the family is otherwise eligible: if there is anyone in the household who is unrelated by blood or marriage to anyone else, *no* food stamps are available. In *United States Department of Agriculture v. Moreno,* the Supreme Court held that, through this law, Congress had violated the Due Process Clause of the Fifth Amendment.[48] It ruled that this law was entirely irrational—perhaps motivated by animosity to hippie communes but, in any event, irrational. The purpose of Congress in this context was to meet nutritional needs. There is no rational relationship, said the Court, between meeting those needs and insisting on a certain kind of relationship between people who happen to live together.

That is where the law stood until 1986, when the Supreme Court again considered a constitutional challenge to a food stamp eligibility rule. This time it faced a congressional scheme that treated unrelated individuals living together *more favorably* than related individuals. In the case of *Lyng v. Castillo*[49] the Court held that Congress did indeed have a rational basis for giving less food stamp money to families than to unrelated cohabitants: families are more likely to dine together, and since food costs are "cheaper by the dozen," they do not need as large a subsidy. Although the majority saw the classification at issue in *Castillo* as qualitatively different from the one in *Moreno,* Justice Marshall, in a dissenting opinion joined by Justice White, argued that the new result could not be squared with the earlier *Moreno* holding.[50]

But even if the *Moreno* case were given a broad reading, the example we have hypothesized is a bit different from that in the food stamp decisions. In *Moreno,* Congress was essentially *starving* people out unless they conformed their living patterns to the requisite national norm. In our example, no one is being deprived of nutrition. No one is being told, "We'll kick you out of public housing, or we won't let you eat, if you don't comply." Every family is being told, regardless of circumstance, that they must eat together once a month. If they don't, perhaps they will be fined, or subject to a prison sentence. This general requirement can't be said to be quite as vicious, quite as irrational; the purpose of this law isn't nutrition: it is family togetherness as such.

But that really does bring us to the heart of the matter. What about the fact that the law invades the realm of family life? Is there anything about *that* which enables us to invoke the Constitution of the United States? True, there is not a word in the Constitution about family or family life. But there is a series of decisions under the Fourteenth Amendment, stretching back to the 1920s, recognizing a realm of autonomy for the family. Nebraska decided that people couldn't have their children learn a modern foreign language; the Supreme Court struck that down in 1923.[51] Oregon enacted a law forbidding parents to send their children to private schools, either religious or military; the Supreme Court struck that down in 1925.[52] Oklahoma determined that certain blue-collar criminals but not white-collar criminals—people repeatedly convicted of ordinary larceny instead of embezzlement—would be sterilized; the Supreme Court held that procreation, although not mentioned in the Constitution, is a fundamental right, and it struck the Oklahoma law down.[53] Connecticut banned the use of contraceptives; in 1965, the Supreme Court in *Griswold v. Connecticut* held that that law, as applied to married couples, was an impermissible invasion into the privacy of the family.[54] In 1967 the Supreme Court held that it is unconstitutional to tell people whom they may and may not marry, striking down Virginia's law against racial intermarriage, in a case aptly named *Loving v. Virginia*.[55] In 1969, the Supreme Court extended the *Griswold* contraception decision to unmarried couples in *Eisenstadt v. Baird*.[56] In 1973, the Court extended these precedents to protect a woman's right to obtain an abortion, in *Roe v. Wade*.[57] These cases, sometimes described as establishing a "right to privacy," are surely relevant to our hypothetical family togetherness ordinance.

One case within this line seems particularly germane. In 1977 a prosecutor in East Cleveland, Ohio, threatened to put a grandmother in jail for living with her two grandchildren because, under the family-law zoning code of East Cleveland, a grandparent could live with two grandchildren only if they were siblings, and these two happened to be *cousins*. The mother of one of the grandsons had died when he was one year old; he had nowhere else to live, so his grandmother took him in. The city told his grandmother, in effect: "Kick him out or go to jail!"

The Supreme Court, in *Moore v. City of East Cleveland,* struck that law down under the Fourteenth Amendment.[58] That's the good news. The bad news is that the decision was five to four. And why not? The Constitution says nothing about grandmothers, parents, children, or family—it doesn't even mention the word *privacy*. In fact, as the Supreme Court's 1989 abortion decision illustrates, there is a mounting attack on that entire *line* of decisions.[59] They are all grounded on notions of family privacy, family autonomy, reproductive freedom, and marital choice that simply are not mentioned in the Constitution.

What, then, of the "tacit postulates" of the constitutional plan? Perhaps we can use those to invalidate the mealtime togetherness ordinance, citing none other than Justice Rehnquist, dissenting in *Nevada v. Hall*.[60] But we have argued that he went too far in abandoning the text in that case; without the Republican Form

Clause, we might have concluded that there is no constitutional basis for protecting states' rights in our first hypothetical case. However rhetorically effective the ploy might be, it won't do to fight fire with fire by adopting methods that we find unacceptable. If the *best* argument one could make from our Constitution is to say that somewhere, somehow there *must* be a tacit postulate ensuring that grandmothers don't get thrown into jail for living with the wrong grandchildren, shouldn't we say that we need a constitutional amendment to protect grandmothers? This is sobering because it is so difficult to amend the Constitution: since the enactment of the Bill of Rights, of the thousands of proposed amendments only sixteen have been ratified. But that by itself does not entitle us to protect grandmothers under *this* Constitution.

Fortunately, the assertion that "it must be somewhere in the Constitution" is *not* the best available argument. For here we *do* have a text: the Due Process Clause of the Fourteenth Amendment. It says that "[n]o State shall . . . deprive any person of life, liberty, or property, without due process of law." Despite continued criticism by original-intent theorists like former federal judge Robert Bork—who maintains that, whenever it interprets the term *liberty* to protect minority rights against majority sentiment, the Supreme Court "legislate[s] at will"[61]—for a very long time the Supreme Court has interpreted this clause to require at least *some* substantive protection as well as protection for fair procedure. Indeed, as recently as 1987 the Court unanimously invoked the doctrine of substantive due process. In *Turner v. Safley,* all the justices agreed that "the decision to marry is a fundamental right," and struck down a near-total ban on marriage by prison inmates.[62] And although some justices periodically question the Court's legitimacy in this area, none seems prepared to eliminate the Court's role in defining the content of liberty, as was illustrated in a 1990 case concerning a prisoner's "liberty interest in avoiding the unwanted administration of antipsychotic drugs under the Due Process Clause of the Fourteenth Amendment."[63]

Indeed, the 1990 "right-to-die" decision indicates that the Supreme Court continues to read the Due Process Clause to limit state interferences with unenumerated fundamental liberties. Prior to 1990 the Court had never faced a claim that there is a constitutional right to die. In *Cruzan v. Missouri Department of Health*, the Court upheld Missouri's rule requiring clear and convincing evidence of a patient's wish not to receive life-sustaining treatment for such treatment to be terminated.[64] Since the Missouri courts had not found such clear and convincing evidence, the result in the particular case was that the state was permitted to keep Nancy Cruzan "alive" in a vegetative state. But in the course of reaching that result, Chief Justice Rehnquist's majority opinion explicitly left open the possibility that a state rule requiring life-sustaining treatment despite a clear expression by the patient that she would not have wanted such treatment would violate the unenumerated constitutional right to die.[65] And Justice O'Connor joined the majority opinion only on the express condition that it recognized such a right.[66] Thus, if one adds her vote to those of the four dissenters, there was a majority of five justices in the *Cruzan* case who read the Due Process Clause to protect the right to die. Depending upon how the other justices in the majority would treat the question that Chief Justice Rehnquist left open, there may be as many as eight votes for this right. Only Justice Scalia, who claimed that using the Due Process Clause in this way enables the Court "to create [rights] out of nothing," explicitly rejected a constitutional right to die.[67]

Returning to our hypothetical case, it seems that under current Supreme Court doctrine, the constitutional line of attack most likely to succeed would argue that there is a fundamental right of individuals to structure their family interactions as they see fit, and that this law impedes that right without serving a compelling government interest. We shall revisit the subject of fundamental rights, and the difficulties inherent in the process of defining their scope, in Chapters 3 through 5.

If we continue to examine the constitutional text we will find another portion of the Fourteenth Amendment helpful: "No State shall make or enforce any law which shall abridge the privileges or immunities of citizens of the United States." It is true that, back in 1873, in the *Slaughterhouse Cases,* the Court emptied that language of nearly all its meaning.[68] The Court there held that this clause only protects against state infringement of individual rights that are especially related to the federal structure, such as the right to travel to Washington, D.C., or to present grievances against the federal government—a strained and strange reading indeed.

Yet the history of the Fourteenth Amendment makes fairly clear that the "privileges or immunities" of United States citizenship were not meant to be limited to rights bearing peculiarly on one's relationship to the national government. Indeed, the historical record indicates that the sponsors of the Fourteenth Amendment deliberately chose language that mirrored a clause already contained in Article IV of the Constitution: "The Citizens of each State shall be entitled to all Privileges and Immunities of Citizens in the several States."[69] Because at the time of the adoption of the Fourteenth Amendment the Article IV Privileges and Immunities Clause had been given a broad substantive interpretation, it is not unreasonable to conclude that the ratifiers of the Fourteenth Amendment intended a similar construction for the new clause.[70]

But even if the history of its adoption were opaque, that would not entitle judges to treat the Privileges and Immunities Clause as "a dead letter," as if it were "written in Sanskrit" or obscured "by an ink blot," as Robert Bork has suggested.[71] Such an interpretive approach is, after all, strikingly at odds with the way we lead our daily lives. For instance, if a mother tells her son, "always do the right thing," we would not think it honorable for the son to ignore her words entirely merely because their intended meaning is not crystal-clear. Rather, we would say that in delivering a somewhat vague message, the mother left to her son the task of applying a general principle to concrete unexpected circumstances. The dutiful son would strive to do the right thing, knowing that he will sometimes falter, but knowing also that if he simply abandons the effort to implement his mother's wishes he will surely fail. So too, judges, legislators, and other officials sworn to uphold the Constitution would be derelict in their duty if they were simply to ignore those parts of the document whose meaning is not crystal-clear to them.[72] As we argued in Chapter 1, it is no more legitimate to *subtract* something from the Constitution because it is out of phase with your vision of the overall plan than it is to *add* something that you wish it contained.

Still, some people have been willing to say that the privileges or immunities of United States citizenship include only those rights that are mentioned in the Bill of Rights. Such readers would construe the enumeration of certain rights in the Bill of Rights to deny or disparage others retained by the people. The Framers were afraid the Bill of Rights might boomerang in exactly that way. But these statesmen were farsighted fellows. James Madison, in fact, proposed the Ninth Amendment for just that purpose— to deal with exactly that boomerang.[73] The Ninth Amendment states: "The enumeration in the Constitution of certain rights shall not be construed to deny or disparage others retained by the people."

The Ninth Amendment does not *create* any rights of its own force. Those who talk of "Ninth Amendment rights" are making a kind of categorical error. The Ninth Amendment creates and confers no rights; it is a rule of interpretation. In fact, it is the *only* rule of interpretation *explicitly* stated in the Constitution. It tells each reader: whatever else you're going to do to explain why "liberty" does not include the grandmother's right to live with her grandchild—whatever else you're going to say to conclude that the "privileges or immunities" of national citizenship do not include the right to use contraceptives—you *cannot* advance the argument that those rights are not there just because they are not enumerated in the Bill of Rights.

Many people have avoided relying on the Ninth Amendment, perhaps fearing how much it might unleash. But that is another instance of illegitimate constitutional subtraction. You may not *like* the Ninth Amendment, but it is undeniably part of the Constitution. And it is not obscured by an ink blot. Thus, in 1965 Justice Goldberg, concurring in the Connecticut birth control case, relied on the Ninth Amendment as a rule of construction.[74] In only one other case has a Supreme Court opinion explicitly relied on the Ninth Amendment. That was the 1980 *Richmond Newspapers* case, which involved the issue of whether the First Amendment guarantees the press and the public a right of access to criminal trials.[75] One of us (Laurence Tribe) argued that case in the Supreme Court, relying primarily on the First Amendment. But freedom of speech, as such, is not really involved when the speakers at the trial, including both the prosecutor and the accused, want the trial to occur in private. Freedom of speech does not include the right to hear something that a speaker doesn't want you to hear. It was because of the sense that the freedom of speech argument was not conclusive in *Richmond Newspapers* that the Ninth Amendment argument was included, and three justices went along. Chief Justice Burger, writing for himself, Justice White, and Justice Stevens, treated the Ninth Amendment as supporting the existence of a presumed right of the press and the public to be present at criminal trials.[76] Four other justices agreed that Virginia could not exclude the press and public from the courtroom, but did not base their conclusions on the Ninth Amendment.

So there has never been a Supreme Court *majority* opinion relying on the Ninth Amendment. And, despite its unique place in the Constitution as the only explicit rule of interpretation in that entire document, quite a few people do not take it very seriously. Senator Grassley of Iowa, for example, during the confirmation hearings on Justice Rehnquist's elevation to be Chief Justice, admonished the future Chief: "Do not smile when I refer to the Ninth Amendment." As it happened, Justice Rehnquist wasn't smiling at that point, but the Senator assumed that the Ninth Amendment wouldn't be taken seriously.

Senator Grassley continued: "I would like to focus on . . . the protection of unenumerated rights for just a minute. No specific right is actually mentioned in that amendment as you obviously know. Exactly what specific rights do you think the framers intended to protect under [the Ninth] Amendment?" Justice Rehnquist recalled the concurrence by Justice Goldberg in the *Griswold* case. And he also recalled the case of *Bowers v. Hardwick,* the Georgia sodomy case that had been decided exactly a month earlier.[77] Concerning the *Hardwick* case, Justice Rehnquist said, "[I] forget whether the Ninth Amendment was directly involved, but it was the same type of case."[78] Indeed, it was much the same type of case, and the Ninth Amendment *was* very much involved. Justice Rehnquist concluded his answer to the Senator: "I just feel I can't answer as to my personal views because I have participated in some cases and they are bound to come up again."[79]

Of course, Chief Justice Rehnquist's published opinions make clear where he stands on this issue. He has persistently dissented from the entire line of privacy decisions, and he joined Justice White's majority opinion in the *Hardwick* case, where the Court held that the State of Georgia could criminalize consensual adult

sodomy in private—at least where homosexual conduct was involved—without giving any reason beyond its moral revulsion
to that act.

We shall revisit the *Hardwick* case in the next chapter as an
illustration of how different members of the Supreme Court can
look at the same line of precedent yet draw radically divergent
conclusions by describing the earlier cases at differing levels of
generality. The majority opinion for the Court in that case is
worth pausing over briefly here, however, because it could herald
the overruling of the entire line of privacy decisions going back
to the 1920s. Former Attorney General Meese, in the cover story
about him in a 1986 issue of the *New York Times Sunday Magazine,*
was quoted as saying that the Reagan administration regarded the
Georgia sodomy decision as its major victory of the Supreme
Court's 1985 term—even though it had not been a party to the
case and had filed no brief.[80]

The Reagan administration regarded that ruling as a major
victory because the majority opinion explicitly adopted the theory
that the administration had advanced for overruling *Roe v. Wade*—
the theory that was accepted completely by Justice White in dissent from the 1986 *Thornburgh* case,[81] where the Court refused to
overrule *Roe v. Wade.* The theory was that such unenumerated
rights as privacy really do not deserve much, if any, protection
at all. Justice White, in dissenting from *Thornburgh* and then again
in writing for the majority in *Hardwick,* said that the Court is on
pretty firm ground when it protects rights spelled out in the Bill
of Rights, but when it comes to these unenumerated rights, the
Court really shouldn't do much, because it opens itself to the
accusation that it is just imposing its values on the people of the
United States.[82] The Bush administration advanced a slightly different argument for overruling *Roe v. Wade.* Arguing before the
Supreme Court in the *Webster* case, former Solicitor General and
current Harvard Law Professor Charles Fried suggested that it
would be possible to restrict abortion without undermining the
other privacy rights.[83] Although the Supreme Court did not overrule *Roe v. Wade* in *Webster,* the Court did substantially restrict
the abortion right. At least three justices seem to have accepted
part of Professor Fried's argument. Writing for himself, Justice
White, and Justice Kennedy, Chief Justice Rehnquist criticized the

opinion in *Roe v. Wade* not merely because it imposed values but also because the trimester scheme announced there included "a whole framework, complete with detailed rules and distinctions."[84] This, in the Chief Justice's view, made the *Roe v. Wade* opinion even more like legislation, and therefore less legitimate, than *Griswold* and the other right to privacy cases.[85]

Even if the Supreme Court is not about to overrule all of its decisions recognizing unenumerated constitutional rights, the Court appears ready to allow a substantial erosion of these rights. Is this because Justice White's view is correct? When the Court recognizes unenumerated rights, does it leave itself open to charges of value-imposition and illegitimacy? Certainly the Supreme Court should *always* try to avoid imposing its values on the people. But refusing to recognize a right so as to protect the Court's reputation against such accusations seems very much like what Dean Jesse Choper advocated in the position we criticized in Chapter 1—that the Court shouldn't protect states' rights, and shouldn't protect the separation of powers, because in that way it can build up a store of capital that it can use for some other purpose. It seems plainly illegitimate to read the Constitution from the perspective of maximizing the Court's political clout.

After all, if the Court refuses to protect a particular right of personal privacy on the ground that it is not quite as traditional, not quite as widely approved by the majority, as are the family rights that have been protected from the 1920s through the 1977 grandmother case, then it is effectively giving these unenumerated rights *less* protection than the provisions of the Bill of Rights get. Those provisions protect rights *from* majorities. They are, or at least should be, protected *most* when they are least popular. To say that a right has to have a majority of the country behind it before it receives protection when it is not one of the explicitly enumerated rights is surely to disparage the right *because* it is not enumerated. The word *disparage* is derived from an old French verb meaning "to degrade or dishonour by marrying to one of inferior rank."[86] To say that unenumerated rights deserve protection only when enough people think those rights ought to be protected is to relegate them to a distinctly lower and more suspect status.

The *Hardwick* majority opinion reads like an exercise in the disparagement of unenumerated rights. By a five-to-four vote, the Supreme Court refused to find a right of privacy protective of the sexual activity at issue there. The Court in effect held that the State of Georgia has no obligation to say anything beyond "we find this conduct immoral." Notice that, in contrast to the *Webster* case, the right that was asserted in *Hardwick* cannot be disconnected from the other privacy rights by claiming that its protection requires the Court to engage in illegitimately "legislative" line-drawing. In fact, quite the opposite is true. By deciding as it did in *Hardwick,* the Court itself drew an unstable line between some kinds of privacy and others, not a line turning on the existence of commerce or of coercion or of demonstrable harm but one turning on popular approval.

Even more troubling than the result in *Hardwick* is the Court's failure to offer a reasoned explanation for the line that it drew. The Court ended up drawing a distinction between the traditional intimacies that were protected by the contraception decisions, and the less traditional intimacies—at least when homosexuals were involved—that it regarded as being at issue in the Georgia case. What about the same acts of sodomy involving heterosexuals? It is unclear what the law is in such a case, for the Court thereafter denied review in a case from Oklahoma involving the same acts by people of different sexes.[87]

What emerges is a largely arbitrary fiat. The Court will protect unenumerated, traditional, family-oriented rights, even outside of marriage—as in the case of *Eisenstadt v. Baird*.[88] It will protect such rights even among unmarried teenagers, as in a case from New York, *Carey v. Population Services International,* which invalidated a ban on the sale or distribution of contraceptives to children under age sixteen.[89] But anatomical combinations that do not seem as traditional to the Court will *not* be protected. Somewhere among the "tacit postulates" of the Constitution there is apparently an anatomical catalogue which the Court consults. This seems like the wrong way to go about developing principles of privacy.

Integration without Hyper-Integration

We can make progress toward the *right* way by looking at the relationship among the Constitution's provisions. Without seeking a grand, unified theory, we may usefully ask whether the Constitution's textual commitment to privacy of the home, strongly evidenced by the Third Amendment and the Fourth Amendment, and its textual commitment to freedom of assembly, which the Court has had little difficulty extending to freedom of association under the First Amendment, together create a zone of privacy for associational intimacies in the home—not a zone of total immunity from government regulation, but a zone that the state cannot enter without special justification. This would bring us closer to the real question in the *Hardwick* case—a question whose answer should not depend on which body parts are involved, or on whether the individuals are of the same sex or of different sexes.

So how about our hypothetical case? The city says: "We find it *immoral* for a family not to have at least one meal a month as a family. We find it repellent that they can't get together for at least one meal a month." As a predictive matter, it is probably safe to say that the Supreme Court would strike down that local ordinance. There would be several justices who would wring their hands and probably dissent, but there would be a majority to hold the law unconstitutional. As Thomas Grey wrote in a 1980 article deftly titled "Eros, Civilization, and the Burger Court":

> [T]he Court has consistently protected traditional familial institutions, bonds and authority against the centrifugal forces of an anomic modern society. Where less traditional values have been directly protected, conspicuously in the cases involving contraception and abortion, the decisions reflect not any Millian glorification of diverse individuality, but the stability-centered concerns of moderate conservative family and population policy.[90]

This observation is a realistic one. But the approach Grey describes is not something that deserves to be called constitutional interpretation. We should not read the Constitution as authorizing the Supreme Court to define basic liberties, or the privileges and immunities of national citizenship, by applying the views of the Mayo Clinic or of Planned Parenthood, whether or not one regards those views as socially enlightened.

As we spell out in Chapter 5, one method worthy of the designation "constitutional interpretation" would seek unenumerated rights by drawing on other parts of the text, coupled with history. In a landmark 1962 article about the Ninth Amendment, then Dean Norman Redlich of New York University Law School proposed looking to the *rest* of the Constitution's text to see what *sorts* of unenumerated rights the Framers might have been concerned not to deny or disparage.[91] If we look at the First, Third, and Fourth Amendments, they suggest a tacit postulate with a textual root—namely, that consensual intimacies in the home are presumptively protected as a privilege of United States citizens.

In fact, at least some of the Framers took for granted such "natural rights," as they would have called them, as the right to marry anyone who consents. Francis Hutcheson, father of the Scottish Enlightenment, put it that way in a widely read eighteenth-century tract.[92] And it turns out that James Madison attended a series of lectures by John Witherspoon of Princeton, who was lecturing, based on the work of Hutcheson, about things like the right to marriage. He treated that as a special case of a right to associate if you so incline with any person you can persuade.[93]

Of course we do not mean to suggest that Madison's or anyone else's personal views of what natural rights people have should determine what the Constitution means. We criticized that position in Chapter 1. However, the historical evidence does show that the Supreme Court's modern privacy jurisprudence has not been mere judicial fiat. When linked to the explicit textual protections for the home and for assembly, the background assumptions of the late eighteenth century provide a plausible basis for affirming the Supreme Court's privacy decisions from the 1920s through 1977, and for concluding that *those* decisions are right and that *Hardwick* is wrong.

Hard Cases Don't Always Make Bad Law

What, then, about the hardest case of all? For many, that remains *Roe v. Wade,* upholding a woman's right to end her pregnancy until the fetus is viable. The issue of abortion continues to divide the nation for a wide variety of social, political, and ethical reasons, none of which is depicted entirely accurately when filtered through the lens of the law.[94] But the question whether there is a constitutional right to an abortion is also a profoundly difficult *legal* question. It is worth asking what makes the question especially difficult. It is not the argument that the woman's side of the equation should find *no* protection in the Constitution. Those who have said that the Court just invented the woman's right to bodily integrity out of whole cloth must simply discard most of the legal developments with respect to personal privacy dating to the 1920s.[95] Protecting your ability to control your own body would have to be on anyone's short list of basic liberties or privileges and immunities in our system of government. It took no great leap beyond the 1942 sterilization case and the contraception cases to say that the woman's interest in avoiding what is, after all, *involuntary* pregnancy—a pregnancy she either did not want in the first place or once wanted but no longer wants to continue—is fundamental.[96]

What makes *Roe v. Wade* difficult is, rather, the remaining question: why cannot the state *nonetheless* restrict this fundamental liberty in the interest of protecting the unborn? In doctrinal terms, why isn't that interest "compelling"? It is quite clear, of course, that the Framers of the Fourteenth Amendment did not think of fetuses as persons, entitled to special protection. Indeed, the amendment includes in its definition of "citizens" "[a]ll persons *born* . . . in the United States."[97] But so what? The state can surely take note of the fact that fetuses soon *will* be "citizens," and that some persons *think* of them as already entitled to the protections of personhood. So why cannot a state act on that perception, however controversial it may be?

In *Abortion: The Clash of Absolutes,* one of us argues that part of the answer may lie in the uniqueness of the resulting impositions on women. As a general rule, the law does not require a man to use his body to save the life of another: although all of us would no doubt think it admirable for a father to donate a kidney to save his daughter's life, in no state does the law *require* such a donation against his will. Thus, if the Supreme Court was justified in protecting women from being compelled by law to remain pregnant, the justification should draw support not only from traditional notions of liberty but also from the textual command of equal protection of the laws. Without some such equality argument, *Roe v. Wade* would probably have been unwarranted.[98]

Some would say that because such strong and incommensurable values are arrayed on both sides of the abortion issue, the correct solution is to pass the buck to the states. Why not simply let each state decide for itself? Fetuses would have superior rights in some states; women would have them in others. If the reason for leaving the matter to the states is that there is no fundamental right involved, that could well mean that not only could State X force a woman to carry her pregnancy to term against her will; it also could mean that State Y could force her to *terminate* the pregnancy against her will, as the government does in China. If the Constitution's silence on the balance between the rights of women and those of the unborn means that the entire matter should be resolved by the states, that may be a knife that cuts both ways.

In this entire area, and in all of the related areas that biomedical technology is bound to serve up as problems for the constitutional allocation of decision-making authority—whether with respect to organ transplants, or surrogate parenthood, or the prolongation of life, or the protection of defective newborns—in all of these areas, the constitutional question cannot simply be extracted from the picture and passed to someone else. This is so for two reasons.

First, to decide that a matter should be left for the states to determine *is* a decision. Consider, for instance, the question of whether the Constitution places any limits on a state's power to use the organs of a dead person's body without that person's prior consent. Whatever their views about the advisability of "nonconsensual organ donation" as a matter of policy, many people might be offended by attempts to frame the issue in terms of property rights. We might think that it cheapens the value of life to treat our organs as commodities. Yet a serious argument has been advanced that the prohibition on deprivations of property without due process of law in the Fifth and Fourteenth Amendments, and the prohibition on takings of property without just compensation in the Fifth Amendment, render forced organ donation unconstitutional.[99] To close our ears to such an argument because we are offended by the notion of conceiving the human body as property is not merely to decide not to *discuss* the issue as one of property rights; it is to decide that there is *no* property right in one's body. Similarly, to decide that the fate of fetuses or of women should be left to the local majority in each state is a fateful and an important decision. It might be justified, but it is not a nondecision.

Moreover, leaving a decision to the states merely postpones the question that every state legislator who takes an oath to uphold the Constitution must ask herself or himself: what does the Constitution permit or compel me to do in this area? Does it permit me to override this or that freedom of choice? Does it permit me to decree the death of this or that person or future person?

These are profoundly troubling questions. But as we suggested earlier, the existence of disagreement about them doesn't mean that, in talking about them, we are somehow getting beyond the outer limits of constitutional interpretation. For there is disagreement even at the very core of constitutional provisions. What the difficulty of these issues *does* tell us is that courts would do well to proceed with caution and humility—to avoid the rush to sweeping, global, across-the-board solutions.

It is in this respect that the Supreme Court in hindsight can be criticized for its performance in *Roe v. Wade.* Some part of the attack leveled against the Court after that decision may have been due to its going beyond the facts before it. After all, the record in that case, although one wouldn't know it from reading the Court's opinion, indicated that the woman involved had apparently been the victim of a gang rape (a claim she retracted in 1987), and yet the State of Texas had required even her to carry her pregnancy to term. Surely the Court could have ruled that, in those circumstances, it violated her rights to be forced to remain pregnant; the Court might have left for another day the difficult problems of line-drawing among degrees and sources of involuntariness.[100]

Apart from the advice of going slowly—of proceeding by a common-law method of case-by-case formulation and reformulation—is there anything more that can be said about these tragic choices, these truly difficult puzzles? Perhaps there is. We can urge one another, along with the judges who bear a special responsibility in constitutional matters, to engage in reasoned conversation with as open a set of minds as we can possibly muster. We needn't lament the close divisions within the Court over the most difficult issues. We should instead welcome the opportunity that such divisions create for a dialogue within the Court that is visible outside its walls. A great opportunity is wasted when the justices talk past one another rather than grappling seriously with the divergent premises and perspectives that the nine of them bring to the interpretive mission. As we concluded in Chapter 1, the Constitution *itself* embodies a multitude of irreconcilable differences.

Of course, it is sometimes nice to have a clear majority opinion, and many lawyers and lower court judges are sometimes confused by the multiplicity of voices. Sometimes, as in *Brown v. Board of Education,* it is crucial that the Court speak with unanimity. But there are higher values than the value of clear signals from the top. In a constitutional republic such as our own, one of those higher values is the open ventilation of conflicting views on the meaning of the Constitution, both as a way of engaging the nation in debate and as a way of modeling what such a debate at its best can be.[101]

In the remaining chapters we join the debate over fundamental rights, taking as our point of departure a viewpoint most dramatically espoused by Justice Scalia. Although we criticize his position, we freely admit that our own affirmative view of how to define fundamental liberties is not without its difficulties. The dialogue will continue, for we make no claim to have found a constitutional conversation-stopper.

3

Judicial Value Choice
in the Definition of Rights

IN A JUSTLY FAMOUS dissent from a case striking down a New York law forbidding employment in a bakery for more than ten hours per day or sixty hours per week, Justice Oliver Wendell Holmes wrote that the "Constitution is not intended to embody a particular economic theory."[1] The case was *Lochner v. New York,* the best known of a line of cases striking down progressive federal and state laws as deprivations of liberty without due process, in violation of the Fifth and Fourteenth Amendments. From the late 1890s until 1937, the Supreme Court deployed what became known as the doctrine of "substantive due process" to protect economic liberties, based on the supposition that the Constitution indirectly embodies the tenets of laissez-faire capitalism. In 1937 the Court reversed course, essentially adopting Holmes's view.[2] Ever since then, the Court has upheld laws regulating economic affairs so long as the body that enacted those laws can be said to have had a rational basis for doing so. This "rational basis" standard is highly deferential to legislative action.[3]

But if the Constitution embodies no particular economic theory, why then should it embody a particular theory of personhood—as it apparently must if we are to make sense of the claim that the word "liberty" in the Due Process Clause encompasses the autonomy to decide whether, for example, to engage in sexual intercourse without the risk of bearing a child? Why, in other words, is the liberty to decide whether to carry a pregnancy to term more fundamental than the liberty to work for less than four dollars per hour? Questions of this sort have plagued constitutional law ever since the end of what came to be known, pejoratively, as the *Lochner* era.

This puzzle arises from what we believe to be a misunderstanding of what was wrong with the Supreme Court's laissez-faire constitutionalism. Cases like *Lochner* cannot be described as illegitimate judicial usurpations merely because the Supreme Court was making substantive value choices: it is difficult to imagine a serious approach to the interpretation of vague terms like "liberty" or "property" that does *not* make choices among values. Were this not the case, were there some value-neutral mathematical algorithm of constitutional interpretation, we would not care so deeply about the character of the women and men charged with interpreting the Constitution. What was wrong with *Lochner*—if indeed it was wrong, as most but not all modern constitutional scholars agree it was—must have been that the Court chose the wrong values to enforce, wrong in the sense that complete laissez-faire capitalism was neither required by the historical understanding of "liberty," nor did it meaningfully enhance the freedom of the vast majority of Americans in the industrialized age, particularly after the onset of the Great Depression.[4]

Constitutional value choices cannot be made, however, without recourse to a system of values that is at least partly external to the constitutional text, since neither the liberty to decide whether to carry a pregnancy to term nor the liberty to work for less than four dollars per hour is explicitly mentioned in the Constitution. The value system that prefers the former liberty to the latter may be one that is widely held among judges or even society in general, but that does not change the fact that it is external to the literal text of the Constitution. How then does a reader of the Constitution discern the contours of the unenumerated rights we discussed in Chapter 2 without imposing her own economic, social, and political theories on the document? How, in other words, does the Constitution *channel* value choice?

Drawing what we have described as the wrong lesson from the *Lochner* era, some people take the fact that protection of a right not explicitly mentioned in the Constitution requires judges to make significant value judgments to mean that the entire exercise of protecting unenumerated rights is illegitimate. To quote but one original-intent theorist, former federal judge Robert Bork has written that heightened judicial scrutiny of laws that harm "discrete and insular minorities"[5] means "that the Justices will read into the Constitution their own subjective sympathies and social preferences."[6] No doubt Bork is correct at least in a limited sense: because the justices of the Supreme Court are human, they are incapable of isolating themselves from the sympathies that move them, and those irreducibly subjective sympathies and preferences are shaped by society.

However, it is one thing to recognize the limits of human objectivity; it is quite another to abandon the effort to approximate it. If taken seriously, Bork's view would do much more than take the Supreme Court out of the business of enforcing *unenumerated* rights: it would require that virtually *no* claim of constitutional right ever be upheld. For in any given case the putative right-holder makes a claim that her specific conduct is constitutionally protected, despite the inevitable fact that the Constitution's text will not describe the details of that conduct.

For example, the Sixth Amendment guarantees a criminal defendant's right to a "speedy" trial. Suppose that because of docket crowding, criminal defendant Jones, unable to post bail, languishes in jail for three years before he is tried for murder. Has he been denied his constitutional right to a speedy trial? If the Court so holds, Bork's view implies that what the Court has done is to create a right: the right to a trial in less than three years is not, after all, enumerated in the Constitution. How is the judgment that three years (or three decades, or three months) is not "speedy" any less subjective than the judgment that the right to have sex without children is part of the "liberty" protected by the Fourteenth Amendment?

In recent years, many scholars of the political left have also made the case that the lines drawn by traditional legal doctrine are sufficiently malleable to allow judges to impose their own values. Among the most commonly voiced opinions of such scholars is the claim that the traditional distinction between the "private" and "public" realms is an artificial one.[7] Such distinctions are criticized from the left as the "product of hegemony and reification."[8] It is worth noting the similarities between these left-wing criticisms and the charges by original-intent theorists that interpretation of words like "liberty" allows unbridled judicial value-imposition. Both the right and the left survey contemporary American jurisprudence and conclude that there is no difference between law and politics. But whereas theorists of the left argue that under the current system the values served are inherently conservative, theorists of the right argue that through self-imposed judicial restraint, judges can avoid imposing their own values.

Thus, for example, Judge Bork contrasts the judicial enterprise of categorizing fundamental rights included within the term "liberty" with that of delineating the boundaries of the rights enumerated in the Bill of Rights. The former enterprise, because it employs such formulas as "deeply rooted in this Nation's history and tradition,"[9] he labels "pretty vaporous stuff."[10] However, the line-drawing necessary to interpret the Bill of Rights, according to Bork, "starts from a solid base, the guarantee of freedom of speech, of freedom from unreasonable searches and seizures, and the like."[11] But Bork does not explain in what way the words "speech" and "unreasonable" are more "solid" than is the phrase "deeply rooted"—or, for that matter, more solid than the word "liberty." Nor, as the speedy trial example illustrates, is there an inherent difference between the two interpretive enterprises.

Perhaps, then, neither the right to have sex without children nor the right to a criminal trial within three years of indictment is actually protected. Would it reduce the Constitution to a nullity to say that only flat contradictions of its literal terms are to be struck down? At times, it's true, cases arise in which constitutional rights may be defined as the mirror images of the text's express prohibitions. Consider, for example, the remarkable city ordinance in *Board of Airport Commissioners for the City of Los Angeles v. Jews for Jesus, Inc.,*[12] which banned "all First Amendment activities" in the Los Angeles airport. Unsurprisingly, the Supreme Court held that the ordinance contravened the First Amendment. But if we really require literal contradictions of the Constitution's terms, even the Los Angeles ordinance could be viewed as constitutional. It did not, after all, purport to ban *all speech,* but only those "First Amendment activities" that take place *in the Los Angeles airport.* And it was not, of course, an enactment of Congress, which alone is expressly bound by the First Amendment's prohibitions. One is hard-pressed to imagine a statute whose judicial invalidation is truly *compelled* by the literal terms of the Constitution. Perhaps the literalist would have to strike down an Act of Congress that made any exercise of "the freedom of speech" punishable by a federal prison term. But then one would have to recall that judicial review is itself an extra-textual practice.

However, unwilling to eliminate the Supreme Court's function of enforcing the Constitution in this way, adherents of a philosophy of judicial restraint generally admit that in spelling out the meaning of vague constitutional phrases, justices must indeed look beyond the Constitution. Their arguments then focus on how the justices are constrained in where they may look. Rather than simply substitute her own values and policy preferences for those of the legislature, they argue, the justice must deploy a value-neutral method of giving specific content to the Constitution's vague terms.[13] Some have claimed that the jurisprudence of original intent, which we discussed in Chapter 1, is such a value-neutral method.[14]

But of course no judge would describe her own enterprise as the substitution of her value judgments for those of the legislature. Instead, lawyers and judges alike will argue, as we did in Chapter 2, that the Constitution itself marks certain values as special. Given his other published views, an unlikely but nonetheless truly eloquent spokesman for this approach was former Judge Bork himself, in his concurrence in *Ollman v. Evans*.[15] Over the dissent of then-Judge Scalia, in a case that expanded the scope of First Amendment protection against libel actions, Judge Bork distinguished the enterprise "of creating new constitutional rights" from that of attempting "to discern how the framers' values, defined in the context of the world they knew, apply to the world we know."[16]

When a judge writes about "the central value" of this or that clause of the Constitution, as Judge Bork did in the *Ollman* case, he suggests that there is a middle ground between the literal text of the Constitution and the purely subjective realm of the judge's own values.[17] As we remarked earlier, one way to go about identifying the central value or values implicit in a specific constitutional clause is to locate that clause within the overall structure of the rest of the Constitution—to ask whether the practices that are either mandated or proscribed by the Constitution presuppose some view without which these textual requirements are incoherent.

Looking to the Framers' Overall Philosophy

Consider, for example, the question of whether the Constitution presupposes any limits on the government's power to define the word "property." During the first half of this century, a school of thought called legal realism emerged which argued, among other things, that the institution of private property was entirely a creation of the law—that what makes an object yours rather than your neighbor's is not any metaphysical relationship between you and the object, but the government's willingness, under certain conditions, to use force to prevent your neighbor from appropriating that object.[18] The legal realists were tremendously influential, and in many ways their program changed the way lawyers of nearly all ideological persuasions think.

But a reader of the Constitution who is persuaded by the realist critique would still act illegitimately were she to conclude that when the Constitution uses the term "property" it refers only to the sum total of that which the government designates as property. This is because, contrary to legal realist theory, the Fifth Amendment's Takings Clause presupposes that property can be prepolitical. The Takings Clause provides that "private property [shall not] be taken for public use, without just compensation." If, as the legal realists argued, property were *only* the sum total of legislative entitlements, then it could never be "taken" because, by definition, that which the legislature declares no longer to be yours would not qualify as private property in the first place.

The Takings Clause, unlike many of the other provisions of the Constitution, really does invite the reader to give special consideration to the Framers' views. A modern legal realist who wants to make sense of the Takings Clause must ask herself: how *could* property be prepolitical in origin? Since her own theory of property cannot answer this question, it would make sense to look at the prevailing political theories of the late eighteenth century, when the Fifth Amendment was written and ratified. Undoubtedly, one of the most influential thinkers for American statesmen of that era was the seventeenth-century English political philosopher John Locke. In his *Second Treatise on Government,* Locke spelled out a natural rights theory of the origin of private property. He started from the premise that in the state of nature every person has a right of property in his or her own body, from which it follows, Locke claimed, that every person also has a property right to the product of the mixture of his or her labor with the natural resources of the earth.[19] According to Locke, property is not merely created by the state's decision to protect what it deems property: property exists prior to the state. Whether or not a modern reader thinks that Locke's theory is a sensible one, something like it is necessary to make sense of, and therefore give content to, the Takings Clause.

Looking to Precedent

Although the constitutional text, as filtered through a reigning political philosophy, will sometimes provide guidance as to an acceptable range of readings, it will not settle most cases. Only a small fraction of a typical twentieth-century opinion interpreting the more familiar clauses of the Constitution will be devoted to the literal constitutional text itself, or to the theories of the Framers. Instead, the elaboration of constitutional values proceeds mostly from prior decisions. Of course, arguments from precedent constitute only one type of constitutional argument. Harvard Law Professor Richard Fallon has remarked that "most judges, lawyers, and commentators recognize the relevance of at least five kinds of constitutional argument: arguments from the plain, necessary, or historical meaning of the constitutional text; arguments about the intent of the framers; arguments of constitutional theory that reason from the hypothesized purposes that best explain either particular constitutional provisions or the constitutional text as a whole; arguments based on judicial precedent; and value arguments that assert claims about justice or social policy."[20] By focusing on arguments from precedent—intended here to include the rationales of prior cases as well as their holdings— we do not deny that other factors play a significant role in constitutional adjudication. We single out precedent-based arguments because such arguments generally take account of these other factors.

Thus, even the boldest innovations in constitutional law have generally been based upon precedent. For instance, in the most famous footnote in constitutional law, Justice Stone argued that state-sanctioned discriminatory practices against "discrete and insular minorities" are entitled to a diminished presumption of constitutionality not because he happened to dislike such discrimination, nor even because the structure of the Constitution marks discrete and insular minorities as special.[21] Instead, he located this principle in prior cases.[22]

One might usefully ask why precedent should matter so much.[23] The usual response—that the law values certainty—seems inadequate given the Court's willingness to depart from precedent, sometimes quite rapidly, when it views a particular precedent as fundamentally unsound.[24] Moreover, concentration on precedent tends to overemphasize the role of the Supreme Court, the least accountable branch of government. Certainly there are other significant constitutional actors whose words and deeds shape our constitutional understanding. As Yale Law Professor Bruce Ackerman has powerfully argued, it has sometimes been the case in American history, as it was during the New Deal, that the structure of the Constitution is in effect altered by the combined actions of Congress and the President.[25]

Perhaps the best answer that can be given is an institutional one: the Supreme Court, as a court, is most properly trusted to read cases, especially its own cases. Right or wrong, it is primarily in the interpretation of prior cases that the battle for constitutional meaning is joined.

But interpretation of prior cases is no simple task. To illustrate, we focus here and in the remaining chapters on one important aspect of the quest for constitutional meaning: how to determine whether a particular right is, in constitutional parlance, "fundamental." To designate a right as fundamental is to require that the state offer a compelling justification for limitations on that right. The Supreme Court has deployed this notion of fundamental rights for two distinct but related purposes. Under the Equal Protection Clause of the Fourteenth Amendment, state-sanctioned inequalities that bear upon the exercise of a fundamental right will be upheld only if they serve a compelling governmental interest.[26] In addition, the designation of a right as fundamental requires the same stringent test for justifying state limitations on the exercise of that right.[27] When the Supreme Court considers a challenge to a law that involves a fundamental right in one of these two ways, it subjects the law to so-called strict scrutiny. With very few exceptions,[28] such "strict" scrutiny is usually "fatal"[29] in fact. Thus, whether to designate a right as fundamental poses perhaps the central substantive question of modern constitutional law.

Levels of Generality

How should the Court go about reading the Constitution to determine if an asserted right is fundamental? Even when prior cases explicitly designate a right as fundamental, limitations of space as well as the institutional limitations on the Court embodied in Article III's case or controversy requirement will mean that those prior cases will not have spelled out the precise contours of the right designated as fundamental. The question then becomes one of characterization: *at what level of generality should the right previously protected, and the right currently claimed, be described?* The more abstractly one states the already-protected right, the more likely it is that the claimed right will be protected under its rubric. For instance, was the right recognized in *Griswold v. Connecticut* the rather narrow right to use contraception, or the broader right to make a variety of procreative decisions? Obviously, the descriptive choice will affect how other cases—for example, those involving abortion—are decided.

It might seem obvious that the selection of a level of generality will necessarily involve value choices. Nonetheless, in the case of *Michael H. v. Gerald D.,*[30] Justice Scalia, writing for himself and Chief Justice Rehnquist, argued that he had discovered a value-neutral means for selecting the appropriate level of generality. The way to select a level of generality, he wrote, is to examine "the most specific level at which a relevant tradition protecting, or denying protection to, the asserted right can be identified."[31] He implied that any other method is arbitrary. We shall have more to say about Justice Scalia's provocative suggestion in Chap-

ter 5, but for now let us explore the scope of this question of
how abstractly to define rights.

To see the centrality of the levels of generality question to the
specification of constitutional rights, consider again the case of
Bowers v. Hardwick, discussed in Chapter 2.[32] Writing for the
majority, Justice White began his discussion with the assertion
that "[t]he issue presented is whether the Federal Constitution
confers a fundamental right upon homosexuals to engage in sodomy."[33] In dissent, Justice Blackmun objected that the case was

> no more about "a fundamental right to engage in homosexual
> sodomy" . . . than *Stanley* [*v. Georgia,* 394 U.S. 557 (1969)] was
> about a fundamental right to watch obscene movies, or *Katz v.
> United States,* 389 U.S. 347 (1967), was about a fundamental right
> to place interstate bets from a telephone booth. Rather, this case
> is about "the most comprehensive of rights and the right most
> valued by civilized men," namely, "the right to be let alone."[34]

As Jed Rubenfeld has noted, Justice Blackmun may have over-
stated the point, since *Katz,* a Fourth Amendment case, involved
a *type* of "privacy" that "does make the claimant's substantive
conduct irrelevant; at issue [in a case like *Katz*] is the government's
manner of discovering the conduct."[35] But it is no less an over-
statement to say, as Rubenfeld did, that Justice Blackmun's "statement . . . was plainly wrong,"[36] for the case need not have been
regarded as one about "homosexual sodomy" at all. Indeed, as
we noted earlier, the state statute that *Hardwick* challenged drew
no distinction between homosexual and heterosexual intimacies.

Clearly, the argument between the majority and the dissent in
Hardwick is an argument over how abstractly to describe the rights
at issue. The majority describes the right claimed by Hardwick
narrowly, the dissent broadly. These alternative descriptions evidently reflect the fact that the majority and the dissent have
reached different conclusions concerning whether Hardwick's behavior is constitutionally protected. As such, we might view them
as shorthand for the holding and the dissent. Yet the characterizations are the starting points for the analysis. Since the majority
and the dissent ask different questions, it is not surprising that
they give different answers.

The question posed by the majority answers itself. To describe a claimed right in very specific terms—here, as a "right to engage in homosexual sodomy"—is to disconnect it from previously established rights. As the majority viewed the issue, the cases on which Michael Hardwick relied were inapposite because they did not deal with the specific right which the majority stated he was claiming. The majority pigeonholed the earlier cases to ensure that no right to privacy broad enough to encompass Michael Hardwick's behavior would emerge: *Pierce v. Society of Sisters* and *Meyer v. Nebraska* were classified "as dealing with child rearing and education";[37] *Prince v. Massachusetts*[38] "with family relationships";[39] *Skinner v. Oklahoma*[40] "with procreation";[41] *Loving v. Virginia* "with marriage";[42] *Griswold v. Connecticut* and *Eisenstadt v. Baird*[43] "with contraception";[44] and *Roe v. Wade* "with abortion."[45] The Court did acknowledge that there was a more abstract right connecting these last three cases, but it described that right as "a fundamental individual right to decide whether or not to beget or bear a child."[46] This right did not encompass a right to engage in homosexual sodomy.

The dissent's initial formulation of the issue is equally conclusory. If the fundamental right protected as "liberty" and established in prior cases is indeed "the right to be let alone," as the dissent at first suggests, then of course the Georgia statute is unconstitutional, or at least triggers strict scrutiny, since far from leaving people like Michael Hardwick alone, it brands them as criminals. But a right to be let alone is manifestly inadequate as a constitutional rule of decision. A right to be let alone while doing what? While harming others? "Harming" others in what way? As determined by whom? These questions make clear the need for a less abstract formulation of the right at stake, and indeed the dissent provided one. The fundamental right that the dissent would have recognized "is the fundamental interest all individuals have in controlling the nature of their intimate associations with others."[47]

Thus, although both the *Hardwick* majority and dissent began from question-begging formulations of the issue at stake, each arrived at a characterization of the prior cases that is at least arguably reasonable. But their characterizations gave strikingly differing results. One fundamental right—to make decisions about family, marriage, or procreation—did not protect Hardwick's conduct. The other right—to control the nature of one's intimate associations—did.

Before addressing the relative merits of these competing abstractions, it is worth considering an important caveat that must accompany any discussion of levels of generality. Although we have described the enterprise of designating fundamental rights as a question of how abstractly to portray rights, we do not wish to imply that there is a single dimension along which abstraction can be measured. A right may be broad along one dimension, while narrow along another. (We shall have more to say about this pervasive feature of the levels of generality question in Chapter 5, where we consider Justice Scalia's claimed solution to it.) For example, as applied to the facts before the Court in *Hardwick,* the right identified in the prior cases by the majority is less abstract (narrower) than the right identified by the dissent. That is, unlike the right to decide whether to beget a child, the right to control intimate associations presumably includes a right to control intimate sexual associations with members of the same sex.

However, there are cases where the majority's right would be broader. Consider, for example, a woman's asserted right to utilize a sperm bank, or to make a surrogate motherhood contract. Under the majority's formulation, these rights are fundamental: the decision to undergo anonymous artificial insemination is a decision to bear a child, and the decision to supply an ovum for laboratory fertilization and subsequent incubation by a "surrogate mother" is a decision to reproduce without incurring the burdens of pregnancy. But the fundamental liberty protected by the *Hardwick* dissent would not protect the right to use a sperm bank or the right to use a surrogate—since the exercise of such rights would reflect decisions to beget a child *without* any intimate association.

How are we to choose between competing abstractions? We may gain some insights into this problem by considering a related puzzle: what is the connection among the rights protected within the Bill of Rights? One answer was suggested by Justice Harlan in his dissent in *Poe v. Ullman.*[48] The liberty protected by the Due Process Clause of the Fourteenth Amendment, he wrote,

> is not a series of isolated points pricked out in terms of the taking of property; the freedom of speech, press, and religion; the right to keep and bear arms; the freedom from unreasonable searches and seizures; and so on. It is a rational continuum which, broadly speaking, includes a freedom from all substantial arbitrary impositions and purposeless restraints . . . and which also recognizes, what a reasonable and sensitive judgment must, that certain interests require particularly careful scrutiny of the state needs asserted to justify their abridgment.[49]

Justice Harlan was engaged in a process of interpolation and extrapolation. From a set of specific liberties which the Bill of Rights explicitly protects, he inferred unifying principles at a higher level of abstraction, focusing at times upon rights instrumentally required if one is to enjoy those specified, and at times upon rights logically presupposed if those specified are to make much sense. An example of the former kind of right would be the right to own a typewriter or word processor, which is instrumentally required for freedom of the press and free speech to flourish—and for that reason was denied throughout much of Eastern Europe until recently. Conversely, some minimal core of private property that cannot be defined away by the government, as discussed earlier, would constitute a right logically presupposed by the Takings Clause of the Fifth Amendment.

Although the immediate concern in *Poe* was a criminal ban on the use of contraception, the method Justice Harlan used is broadly applicable. Suppose, for example, that the government were to conspire with the television networks to include subliminal messages urging viewers to "return the Administration to office" in key broadcasts during the fall before a national election. Would your right to freedom of speech have been violated? The literal terms of the First Amendment do not prohibit such messages, but Justice Harlan's point was that the freedom of speech, the freedom of religion, and so forth make sense only if connected by a broader and underlying principle of freedom of thought and conscience. Moreover, by proposing that rights should be perceived to lie on what he called a *rational* continuum, Justice Harlan indicated that they make more sense if abstracted from the particular spheres of life they protect. Free speech is an empty freedom if not possessed by a free mind.

The lesson of Justice Harlan's *Poe* dissent applies no less to the enterprise of connecting cases than it does to that of connecting clauses of the Constitution. His lesson is that, if constitutional decision making is to be in any sense "rational," then one must seek rationalizing—that is, unifying—principles to link disparate decisions. To the extent that it coheres with our experience to view decisions about child rearing and family, decisions about marriage, and decisions about procreation as concerning completely isolated areas of life—as did the *Hardwick* majority—we will not seek an underlying unifying principle. However, if presumptively excluding government from these areas of life appears to be a connected project—if these freedoms appear to be different manifestations of the same underlying liberty to control the nature of one's intimate associations—then we might well connect the "points" of liberty in the way the *Hardwick* dissenters did.

It might be argued that the *Hardwick* majority did connect the points, but in a different way. Perhaps the Court had in mind an underlying if unarticulated unifying principle: protection of the traditional nuclear family. However, this principle explains too little, for, as the *Eisenstadt* case illustrates, reproductive freedom is constitutionally guaranteed to single mothers no less than to married ones, and as *Moore v. East Cleveland*—the grandmother case we discussed in Chapter 2—held, the right to familial association extends beyond the traditional nuclear family. Nor could a line drawn around the nuclear family be plausibly connected with constitutional text, structure, or history.

On more than one occasion the Supreme Court has failed to recognize the relationship between liberties which upon reflection seem quite closely linked. Consider, for example, one area of the law that has been characterized by quite artificial boundaries: the scope of First Amendment protection afforded to various media. In *Kovacs v. Cooper*,[50] the Court upheld a city ordinance banning the use of sound trucks on the public streets as a valid time, place, and manner restriction. The result is hardly disturbing, as anyone who has ever been annoyed by a loud sound truck will probably agree. However, there is a remarkable statement contained in

Justice Jackson's concurrence. Emphasizing the narrowness of the holding, he distinguished sound trucks from movies, radio, and other media. "Each" medium, Justice Jackson claimed, "is a law unto itself, and all we are dealing with now is the sound truck."[51] Justice White expressed a similar sentiment more than thirty years later in *Metromedia, Inc. v. San Diego,*[52] a case involving a challenge to San Diego's billboard ordinance. After perfunctorily acknowledging that the First Amendment contains broad principles, he defined his task narrowly: "[w]e deal here with the law of billboards."[53]

The claim that there is a unique body of law applicable to each medium of expression is false both as a descriptive and as a normative matter. Were there really a unique law of billboards, distinct from the law of sound trucks and other media, there would be no reason for the authors of the *Kovacs* and *Metromedia* opinions to have considered cases dealing with other media, and to their credit, they did at least cite some such cases.

Moreover, to segregate the reasoning applicable to one medium from the reasoning that has prevailed in other media would be irrational. What, for example, would such a program do with a new medium? Must there be a unique "law of compact discs" distinct from the prior "law of phonograph records"? For that matter, how abstractly are we to define a medium? Is there a "law of Betamax VCRs" distinct from the "law of VHS VCRs"? To what sources does one turn to infer the "law of fax machines"? If judges can consult neither general principles of First Amendment law nor prior historical traditions—for, by definition, there will be no historical traditions regarding a *new* medium—they will be completely at sea. In this way, the capacity to generalize serves not as a source of judicial subjectivity but as a limit upon it.

In opposition to the radical reductionism exemplified by the reasoning of opinions like *Hardwick* and *Metromedia,* Justice Harlan's suggestion in *Poe* challenges us with an admittedly imprecise and indeterminate mission: insofar as constitutional law aspires to be "rational," he says, we should seek unifying principles.

Nonetheless, more than one unifying principle is almost always available. Thus, according to Paul Brest, "[t]he indeterminacy and manipulability of levels of generality"[54] require the Court to make value choices in deciding whether or not to infer a fundamental right from a constellation of precedent and historical social practice. Among the authorities cited by Brest in support of the argument that the selection of an appropriate level of generality is arbitrary is Robert Bork.[55] Brest goes on to note, however, that the indeterminacy of abstraction plagues originalism no less than other interpretive schools. If the Court is not to refer to the Framers' most specific intent—as Bork claims it must not in order to save *Brown v. Board of Education*[56] from being destroyed by the specific views about segregation held by the authors of the Fourteenth Amendment—how can he select a meaning for equality in a value-neutral way?[57]

Bork apparently misapprehends this criticism. In response to Brest, he argues that "[o]riginal understanding avoids the problem of the level of generality in equal protection analysis by finding the level of generality that interpretation of the words, structure, and history of the Constitution fairly supports."[58] In his review of Judge Bork's book on the Constitution, Bruce Ackerman notes that to apply a theory of original intent requires an enormous amount of historical research and analysis of original source material, research which Ackerman argues Bork has not done.[59] But let us assume that someone has done the research and analysis which Ackerman says originalism requires. What then? We contend that a quest for the "original understanding"—or for that matter, for any all-purpose dictionary of constitutional meaning—will not "avoid[ ] the problem of the level of generality." As we attempt to show in the next chapter, the interpretation of words, structure, and history can usually "fairly support" a wide variety of conclusions. The value-laden *choice* of a level of generality remains.

4

Seeking Guidance from Other Disciplines:
Law, Literature, and Mathematics

WHAT, IF ANYTHING, about the value-laden nature of constitutional interpretation is unique to the law, as opposed to the process
of interpreting any text? Does the process of reading, say, a novel
differ qualitatively from that of reading the Constitution? If so,
is the difference captured by the fact that, as Justice Harlan put
it, constitutional adjudication should be rule-like and *rational?* If
that is true, then should we instead take as our model the process
of constructing a mathematical proof—a proof in accord with
mathematical rules and principles? In this chapter we look outside
the law to literature and mathematics so that we may gain some
perspective on what is unique about reading the *Constitution*.

How Law Is Like Literature

How should a judge faced with a case of first impression apply
prior decisions in cases involving related but different facts? In an
essay titled "How Law Is Like Literature," Ronald Dworkin
draws an analogy between the process of using precedent and the
composition of a chain novel. A chain novel is a book written by
many different authors; each successive author must continue the
story written by those who preceded her. In Dworkin's analogy,
just as the quality of a chain novelist's creation is measured by
how well it builds upon what came before, so the judge's opinion
is evaluated by asking how well it fits in among prior precedent.[1]

As Dworkin himself admits, the analogy is imperfect. For
instance, judges sometimes overrule cases, or confine them to

their facts. Moreover, there is a great deal of disagreement among legal scholars over how lawyers should use the tools of literary theory.[2] For our purposes, however, we shall assume that the analogy is sufficiently close that useful insights about law may be obtained by examining literature.

The most important insight comes from the obvious fact that a story can have more than one ending that is consistent with what has come before. Consider, for example, Charles Dickens's *Great Expectations*. In Dickens's original manuscript, Pip's love for Estella remains forever unrequited. However, on the advice of his publisher, Edward Bulwer Lytton, Dickens changed the ending, uniting the hero and his love. He then published the sanguine version.[3] Which ending fits the story better? Bulwer Lytton—in a position like a chain novelist—judged that Victorian audiences would prefer the happy ending. By contrast, later critics have tended to prefer Dickens's original ending, not so much because it was the original but because their sensibilities were less sentimental than those of the Victorians. For instance, George Bernard Shaw, who edited the novel for a 1937 publication, used the original ending, relegating the other to a postscript for "[s]entimental readers who still like all their stories to end at the altar rails."[4]

A given story, then, can be consistent with more than one ending. What causes one reader to prefer one ending and another reader to prefer a different ending is not consistency in the abstract, but aesthetic value judgments of one sort or another. These value judgments are necessarily external to the text.

Before applying this insight to the general structure of legal decision making, it is worth pausing over the question of what it means to say that a value is external to a text. In one sense, all meaning is external to text: to attribute meaning to a collection of ink marks on paper or vibrations of the air presupposes that the reader or listener has a means for deciphering the linguistic code being used. To someone who does not understand English, *Great Expectations* is meaningless. If we are to give her the tools to understand the novel, we must first teach her English—the rules of which are most certainly external to the novel itself.

This problem is not solved by assuming that we may implicitly append to any text a guide to the language in which it is written.

Because such a guide must itself be decoded, there will remain an irreducible minimum of meaning that the reader will have to supply on her own.[5] People bother to write novels, or to speak to one another, because they accept that they are each supplying the same irreducible meaning. For example, when two people look at the same object and call it an elephant we have no way of knowing that their respective subjective experiences are even remotely similar; yet our belief that we can and do communicate to one another indicates that we assume that there is a common human experience of the world.

Are there similar unspoken extra-textual assumptions about the Constitution without which it makes no sense to speak of it as having a meaning? Since the Constitution is itself a text, all of the assumptions necessary to make sense of any text naturally apply to the Constitution. The question here is whether there are *additional* unspoken assumptions. The answer to that question would appear to be yes. Consider, for example, the widely shared belief that the Constitution is the supreme law of the land. This cannot be true merely because the Supremacy Clause of Article VI *says* that "[t]his Constitution . . . shall be the supreme Law of the Land." Suppose that a group of law professors, dissatisfied with the familiar Constitution, write their own constitution, and that their version also includes a clause declaring *it* to be the supreme law of the land. What makes the former the actual supreme law of the land and the law professors' effort a mere conceit are certain beliefs about political theory and history. The Supremacy Clause is binding to the extent that readers of the Constitution agree that sovereignty derives from the people; that one generation may bind another; and that the Philadelphia Convention of 1787 and subsequent ratification processes were in fact expressions of the national will to create a lasting government.

These unspoken assumptions that give meaning to the constitutional text are more controversial than those that give meaning to language in general. Although we know that we cannot logically refute the solipsist, few of us seriously doubt that there is an external world about which we can actually exchange information. By contrast, many would question the assumptions underlying the legitimacy of the Constitution. Some would deny that democracy, which can degenerate into mob rule, is preferable to enlightened despotism. Others would wonder why the views of long-dead generations should shape our government. Still others would challenge the premise that we should be bound by an instrument that was created without consulting women, slaves, or those without property—that is, the majority of the adult population. Why *should* such premises be accepted?

One answer to questions of this sort is that they are not legal questions at all. Positive law, it might be argued, proceeds from the *axiom* that we all agree that the law to be interpreted is contained in this or that book. According to this view, deciding between the Constitution of 1787 and the 1990 "constitution" of the law professors is a matter for political theorists, not the law. The difficulty with this explanation is that the need to resort to extra-constitutional values is not confined to the question of what the Constitution *is,* but pervades the question of what the Constitution *means.* This question, at least, is a matter for law.

The need to resort to extra-constitutional values in interpreting the Constitution manifests itself strikingly in the fundamental rights question we introduced in Chapter 3. For example, in *Roe v. Wade* the Court was asked to determine whether and under what circumstances a woman's decision to have an abortion is part of the fundamental right to privacy recognized in the contraception cases.[6] Viewed as literature, the majority decision in *Roe* is easy to reconcile with these prior cases. If the story of *Eisenstadt* is one of freedom to avoid motherhood before conception, *Roe* continues the story so as to protect that right for a time after conception.

But can we say that the result in *Roe* was *dictated* by *Griswold* and *Eisenstadt?* Certainly the dissenting view in *Roe* does not make for a story that is necessarily *inconsistent* with the contraception decisions on their own terms. Whether the dissenting opinions themselves are consistent with the prior cases is, of course, a different matter. Justice White concurred in the judgment in *Griswold* because the Connecticut statute there regulated what he deemed a fundamental liberty interest in the marriage relationship.[7] Yet his *Roe* dissent rested in large part on principles of judicial restraint in the face of majority sentiment,[8] principles which should have been equally applicable in *Griswold.*

But even if the rationales underlying Justice White's opinions in the two cases are inconsistent, certainly we can imagine a way to reconcile his positions. According to the story we would tell, conception marks the start of a new chapter. In this story, state legislators are free to restrict abortions, so long as the restrictions meet the minimal requirement of rationality.

To say that the majority and the dissent can each tell consistent stories is not to say that there is no reason to prefer one story over the other. Each side will appeal to what it perceives to be widely shared values. Those who would deny that a right is fundamental will often march under the banner of majoritarianism. Who are we (or you) unelected judges to declare X a fundamental right, they will ask, when so many states do not consider it so? The other side will respond by pointing to all of the rights that have been deemed fundamental in the past despite state efforts to abridge them, and will attempt to locate X within the scope of the previously described rights. And, of course, both sides will make claims about the kind of society that protects or abridges right X. Just as in literature the criteria for judging which ending to a story is preferable are external to the story itself, so in law the criteria for judging whether a fundamental right should be articulated at a sufficiently abstract level to include the claimed right must be derived from some source other than the four corners of the prior opinions. In the case of literature, the external criteria are aesthetic. In law they are political and moral, and, to the extent that the word describes the praxis of lawyers, the criteria will also be legal.

Thus far we have contended that the text of a work of literature up until any given point is indeterminate. It will be consistent with more than one ending. But it will not be equally consistent with all endings. That is, although the internal structure of a text may be consistent with ending A or ending B, surely there are some endings that are simply beyond the pale. Or are there?

Consider again the example of *Great Expectations*. Suppose that in place of either of the final chapters Dickens actually wrote, we rewrite the final chapter as a non sequitur. Pip and Estella are eaten by space aliens. Or Miss Haversham is reincarnated as a giant talking cockroach, while Pip emigrates to Bolivia to become a shepherd. Or why not a final chapter that is totally unconnected with what precedes it? Replace the original final chapter with the final two chapters of *this* book, perhaps translated into Swedish, and delete the references to *Great Expectations*! Surely these endings are inconsistent with the rest of the novel.

But even these bizarre examples are not *logically* ruled out by the prior text. Just as the choice between the original ending and the publisher's amendment came down to aesthetic criteria, so too is the judgment that the endings of the previous paragraph are unacceptable an aesthetic judgment. The difference is that the aesthetic convictions that rule out the non-sequitur endings are widely shared. Most readers will prefer books written in only one language.[9] By contrast, there is likely to be greater disagreement concerning whether tragic endings are more desirable than happy ones. The difference, however, is a matter of degree rather than kind. Indeed, it is also culturally contingent: we can imagine an angst-ridden polyglot nation in which all agree that tragedy is superior to comedy, though the people are deeply divided as to the ideal number of languages in which a book should be written.

In law too, some results will seemingly be ruled out by widely shared beliefs about what makes sense. For example, suppose that *Griswold* had come out the other way. This would seemingly rule out the decision in *Roe*. After all, it would make no sense to say that there is a fundamental right to abort a potential human life after it has been conceived, but not to prevent conception in the first place. Anti-*Roe* seems to follow inexorably from anti-*Griswold*.

But even this judgment is not a matter of pure logic. Concurring in *Thornburgh v. American College of Obstetricians & Gynecologists*,[10] Justice Stevens argued that, as between the decision whether to use contraception and the decision whether to have an abortion, "it is the post-conception decision that is more serious," and therefore implicates an arguably greater liberty interest.[11] Presumably this is so because the decision not to use contraception is a decision to *risk* becoming a mother, whereas the decision not to have an abortion is a decision actually to *become* a mother, and therefore to accept the joys and burdens of motherhood. Although Justice Stevens conceded that in the abortion context there may be a stronger countervailing interest to be weighed against the woman's reproductive freedom, his analysis suggests a not wholly implausible means for reconciling *Roe* with anti-*Griswold*.

Moreover, the judgment that there is a fundamental right to an abortion but not to contraception might be explained by myriad other rules of constitutional decision making. Perhaps the justices secretly adhere to a canon of constitutional construction requiring that fundamental rights begin in vowels: abortion is in, contraception out. Of course no one would actually argue for such a rule, but this fact is merely a matter of consensus. There would be widespread agreement that such a rule of law is arbitrary; yet what is arbitrary and what is salient is itself a cultural matter. In colonial Salem, for instance, a defendant could be convicted of witchery because an examination of her body revealed unusual growths—taken as indicia that she had made a pact with the devil.[12] No doubt this procedure seems arbitrary (and cruel) to us, but it was deemed to provide highly credible evidence in that different place and time.

The comparison with literature shows that the internal structure of prior cases combined with an appeal to widely shared values can rule out some formulations of a fundamental right. The difficulty arises when appeals are made to values that are not shared. And in virtually any interesting case, such conflicting appeals will be available.

How Law Is Unlike Mathematics

The lessons we have drawn from literature might be rebutted by focusing on yet another important way in which law is not like literature. Except in some self-conscious modern works,[13] the author of a piece of literature does not usually attempt to justify his enterprise within the enterprise itself. But that is precisely what judicial opinions do. A judge writes an opinion not merely so that it will in fact fit the prior cases; within the opinion itself she argues *why* it fits the prior cases. The literary analogy does not capture this argumentative element of law. Might the self-referential quality of legal interpretation render law free from the indeterminacy that plagues literary interpretation? To answer this question it will be fruitful to compare the judicial enterprise with another self-justificatory process, mathematical proof. However, we will show that this comparison only reinforces the conclusion that specifying an appropriate abstraction to characterize prior cases cannot be accomplished without making value choices.

What is the nature of mathematical proof? In a very influential work, Imre Lakatos challenged the conventional view of mathematics as the accumulation of proven truths.[14] Instead, Lakatos claimed, mathematics is a process by which proofs are made more rigorous as they are subjected to counterexamples and criticisms. Lakatos's insights have potentially numerous applications to many fields,[15] including law. One of these applications bears upon the abstraction problem. For that reason, we shall briefly set out a schematic description of Lakatos's analysis of mathematical proof.

The Mathematical Enterprise according to Lakatos

Lakatos illustrated his method by a dialogue concerning proof of a theorem about regular polyhedra, namely that for all regular polyhedra, $V - E + F = 2$, where V = the number of vertices, E = the number of edges, and F = the number of faces. Limitations of space, and the recognition that readers of this book may find the excursion into solid geometry daunting, have led us to substitute a somewhat simpler and, we hope, more familiar example. For our limited purposes, no loss of generality results. Consider the following proof, which you may have encountered in high school.

Proposition: The sum of the angles of any triangle is 180°.

Proof:

1. Let a, b, and c be the angles of triangle ABC.

2. Adjacent to ABC draw a similar triangle A'B'C'. Since the triangles are similar, the angle opposite A' will equal angle a, as shown in Figure 1.

3. Let d be the angle between segments A and C'. Since c, d, and a (of triangle A'B'C') form a straight angle, we have a + d + c = 180°.

4. But A is a transversal that cuts parallel segments C and C'. By Euclid's Fifth Postulate, when two parallel lines are cut by a transversal, alternate interior angles are equal. Thus, b = d.

5. Substituting this into our previous equality, a + b + c = 180°, and we have completed the proof.

Now suppose that someone comes along claiming to have discovered a triangle for which the sum of the angles is greater than 180°. Her triangle is drawn on the surface of a sphere. It has

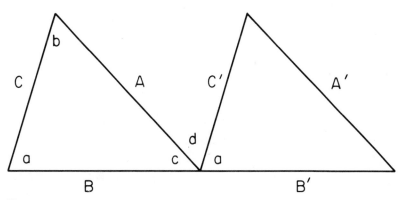

Figure 1

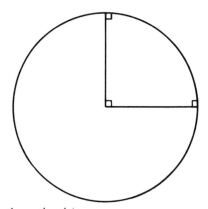

Figure 2 (view from the north pole)

one vertex at the north pole and the other two on the equator, as shown in Figure 2. Each of the angles formed by the intersection of the equator with the other legs is a right angle, so their sum is 180°. Adding the angle at the north pole, we have a sum that is greater than 180°.

What are we to do with the object of Figure 2? Lakatos identifies three approaches that mathematicians typically take when confronted with counterexamples: (1) monster-barring; (2) exception-barring; and (3) lemma-incorporation.

The monster-barring approach, as the name suggests, treats the object of Figure 2 as no counterexample at all. "That is not a triangle at all," says the monster-barrer. "The word *triangle* does not include enclosed areas on the surface of a sphere. Therefore, you haven't provided a counterexample, but a monster. My proof is still valid." The monster-barrer preserves the truth of his theorem by brute force, defining away all challenges.

A more sophisticated (but still flawed) approach is that of exception-barring. The exception-barrer admits that there can be a triangle on the surface of a sphere, and therefore that Figure 2 is indeed a counterexample. Knowing, however, that for a great many triangles the proposition still holds true, the exception-barrer is unwilling to sacrifice it. Consequently, she modifies her proposition to state:

Exception-Barrer's Modified Proposition: For all triangles that are not on the surface of a sphere, the sum of the angles = 180°.

The difficulty with the modified proposition is that we no longer have any confidence in our proof. Because the exception-barrer has modified the proposition in a completely ad hoc manner, we have no understanding of what was wrong with our proof in the first place, nor do we have any guarantee that there aren't more exceptions lurking about.

What is needed, according to Lakatos, is a method that relates the exception to the proof. That method is lemma-incorporation. Because the existence of a counterexample to the proposition means that some step of the proof must be false, the lemma-incorporator searches for that false lemma. In our example, we would find that step 4, which assumed the truth of Euclid's Fifth Postulate, is the suspect step. The Fifth Postulate holds for Euclidean surfaces—indeed, a Euclidean surface is often *defined* as one in which the Fifth Postulate holds—but not for all surfaces, and not for the surface of a sphere. (We leave the verification of this mathematical fact to the interested reader, who should note that on the surface of a sphere, "parallel lines" are great circles that intersect at exactly two points. Hint: Consider a transversal that cuts two great circles near one of their points of intersection.)

The lemma-incorporator now modifies the proposition to state:

Lemma-Incorporator's Modified Proposition: For all triangles on surfaces where Euclid's Fifth Postulate holds, the sum of the angles = 180°.

Lemma-incorporation is superior to exception-barring because the former preserves the original proof. Step 4 of our original proof may now be deployed with complete confidence since we have made its controversial assertion into an explicit assumption. The original proof is valid, but for a limited domain. By the method of lemma-incorporation we have specified that domain of validity.

Lakatos and the Law

We begin our application of Lakatos by examining the equivalent of monster-barring in the legal world. Recall that a mathematical monster-barrer, when faced with a triangle on the surface of a sphere, blithely asserts: "That's not a triangle at all, so my theorem is still true." He attempts to make the counterexample go away by brute force. In the law there is an analogous device called drawing a distinction without a difference.

Consider, for example, the Supreme Court's effort to delineate when the case or controversy requirement of Article III allows a citizen to come into court challenging government action on no other basis than that she has been injured in her capacity as a taxpayer. In *Flast v. Cohen*[16] a taxpayer brought such a suit challenging the expenditure of federal funds to subsidize religious education. The Supreme Court held that the suit was permissible—that in legal terms, the taxpayer had "standing." However, in an apparent fear that the holding might spawn a rash of taxpayer suits, the Court limited the principle to those cases where the taxpayer "allege[s] the unconstitutionality only of exercises of congressional power under the taxing and spending clause of Art. I, § 8 of the Constitution."[17] Sure enough, fourteen years later the Court denied standing in *Valley Forge Christian College v. Americans United for Separation of Church and State*[18] because the challenged action in that case "was not an exercise of authority conferred by the Taxing and Spending Clause of Art. I, § 8 [but] an evident exercise of Congress' power under the Property Clause, Art. IV, § 2, cl. 2."[19] There may well be good reasons to deny taxpayer standing in some cases and allow it in others, but it is difficult to comprehend why anything should turn on the clause of the Constitution pursuant to which Congress exercises power. This is true first because a taxpayer may suffer more through the unconstitutional disposition of property (as in *Valley*

Forge) than through a budgetary expenditure, and second because many acts of Congress are authorized by more than one clause of the Constitution.

The taxpayer standing cases exemplify legal monster-barring insofar as they attempt to cordon off whole areas of law by judicial fiat. Just as the mathematical monster-barrer defines away the non-Euclidean triangle, so the judicial monster-barrer arbitrarily limits the scope of his rule.

Let us now look at another example of legal monster-barring, one suggested by Lakatos himself. Early in Lakatos's dialogue, the monster-barring student asserts that a "woman with a child in her womb is not a counterexample to the thesis that human beings have one head."[20] Returning to the fundamental rights context, we might ask if the right to abortion in *Roe* follows logically from the right to use contraception in *Griswold* and *Eisenstadt*. Is a woman with a fetus in her womb a counterexample to the thesis that human beings have a fundamental right to choose whether or not to have children as a result of having sex? A monster-barrer who wished to retain *Griswold* and *Eisenstadt* while jettisoning *Roe* might argue as follows: because the contraception cases dealt with the liberty to decide whether or not to have sex without children *before* conception, the liberty they deem fundamental is not even implicated by abortion. A monster-barrer characteristically *asserts* that his level of generality is appropriate, without *arguing* why it should not be otherwise. Monster-barring is no more intellectually satisfying in law than in mathematics.

Turning to the next approach to proof, it is easy to see that exception-barring also has an analogue in legal argumentation. Recall that the mathematical exception-barrer adjusts her proposition without examining the associated proof. As a legal analogue, we have in mind those instances when the Court relies on the holdings of prior cases while ignoring their rationales. An example of such a case is *Morrison v. Olson,* the 1988 case that held the special prosecutor law to be constitutional.[21] Former Assistant Attorney General Ted Olson, who was a target of an investigation by special prosecutor Alexia Morrison, challenged the law as a violation of the separation of powers. He argued that the kind of power she exercised could be given only to someone within the President's chain of command. The Supreme Court disagreed, with Chief Justice Rehnquist writing the majority opinion. Only Justice Scalia dissented.

Although the result in *Morrison* is certainly defensible, its treatment of prior cases exemplifies exception-barring. The crucial separation of powers inquiry that the Supreme Court had identified in its pre-*Morrison* cases clearly focused on the nature of the powers given to an official removable by the Executive. Purely executive powers, as opposed to quasi-legislative or quasi-judicial powers, had to be given to someone under the President's supervision.[22] The Court could have upheld the special prosecutor law by concluding that criminal prosecution is not a purely executive power; after all, throughout much of American history private citizens have been able to bring criminal prosecutions. Instead, Chief Justice Rehnquist's opinion simply ignored the rationales of the prior cases and substituted a balancing test: "the real question is whether the removal restrictions [on the office of the special prosecutor] are of such a nature that they impede the President's ability to perform his constitutional duty."[23] The Court found, not surprisingly, that its balancing test produced the same results in the prior cases as had their actual rationales, and then proceeded to apply the test to the case before it.

Although legal exception-barring produces results that are consistent with prior precedents, it does so at the cost of undermining those very precedents. Presumably, one of the reasons for relying on prior decisions in new settings is the belief that the prior decisions were based upon sound reasoning. Thus, when the Court disavows or ignores that reasoning, it weakens the strength of the very precedents upon which it relies.

A particularly egregious example of exception-barring can be seen in the Supreme Court's 1990 decision in *Oregon v. Smith*.[24] In that case, two Native Americans who had been denied state unemployment benefits because they were dismissed from their jobs for using peyote, an illegal drug, claimed that since their religion required them to use peyote for ritual purposes, the denial of benefits violated their First Amendment right to free exercise of religion. The Court held that there was no constitutional denial. En route to reaching this conclusion, the Court did not ask whether the state's interest in criminalizing peyote was sufficiently compelling to justify the burden upon the Native Americans'

religious freedom. Instead, writing for the majority of five justices, Justice Scalia claimed that the Court had "never held that
an individual's religious beliefs excuse him from compliance with
an otherwise valid law prohibiting conduct that the State is free
to regulate."[25] Since the only question was whether the state could
regulate drug use generally—and who would say that it could
not?—the majority did not even consider the case as presenting a
threat to free exercise.

Smith exemplifies exception-barring because Justice Scalia's rationale was based on a self-serving recharacterization of a long
line of cases requiring exemptions from otherwise valid general
state policies where those policies conflicted with religious beliefs.
When children who were Jehovah's Witnesses challenged a man-
datory flag salute law, the Supreme Court ruled in *West Virginia
Board of Education v. Barnette* that while public schools may begin
the school day with a flag salute, they may not compel children
to participate.[26] In *Sherbert v. Verner* the Court held that South
Carolina could not deny a Seventh Day Adventist unemployment
benefits for her refusal to work on Saturday, her Sabbath.[27] This
principle was reaffirmed as recently as 1987.[28] And in *Wisconsin
v. Yoder*[29] the Court held that a state could not compel Amish
children to attend school beyond the eighth grade, notwithstanding the indisputable validity of the state's compulsory education
policy in general.

The Court in *Smith* distinguished *Yoder* and the other cases by
characterizing those cases as involving religion "in conjunction
with other constitutional protections, such as freedom of speech
and of the press, . . . or the right of parents . . . to direct the
education of their children."[30] In light of Justice Scalia's usual
reluctance to recognize unenumerated fundamental liberty interests such as parenthood,[31] it is quite remarkable that he would
choose to characterize *Yoder* as resting not on the explicit textual
protection of free exercise of religion but on an implicit right of
parenthood. But quite apart from this inconsistency, the characterization grossly misstates the rationale of *Yoder* itself, where the
Court explicitly grounded its holding in the fact that there was
no "state interest of sufficient magnitude to override the interest
[claimed by the Amish] under the Free Exercise Clause."[32] Thus,
as with all instances of exception-barring, one is left wondering

what if anything is left of the principles announced in the prior cases.

This weakness of the exception-barring approach was summarized nicely by Justice O'Connor in her opinion in *Smith,* which though concurring in the judgment was harshly critical of the majority's rationale. Objecting to Justice Scalia's characterization of prior religion cases, she noted that the fact that the Court "rejected the free exercise claims in [some of] those cases hardly calls into question the applicability of First Amendment doctrine in the first place. Indeed, it is surely unusual to judge the vitality of a constitutional doctrine by looking to the win-loss record of the plaintiffs who happen to come before" the Court.[33] Justice O'Connor reminds us that although practicing lawyers may be wise to look not to what courts say, but what they do, as a means of *predicting* the outcome of a case, this is hardly an acceptable method for a judge to use in *deciding* a case.

Finally, we turn to Lakatos's preferred method for dealing with counterexamples: lemma-incorporation. Here, however, the analogy between mathematics and law breaks down. To see this, imagine that before the *Hardwick* case has made it to the Supreme Court, Justices B and W are having a discussion. B contends that there is a fundamental right to control the nature of one's intimate associations. He locates this right in the Court's prior privacy decisions. W claims that there is no such right, and offers homosexual sodomy as a counterexample to B's abstraction.

If B were a monster-barrer, he might quote Blackstone for the opinion that homosexual sodomy is a "crime not fit to be named," and therefore conclude that it is no more an intimate association worth protection than is rape.[34] If B were an exception-barrer, he could contend that this is indeed an exception, and without reconsidering how he derived the right, could recharacterize the liberty interest as a fundamental right to control the nature of one's intimate associations, *except for homosexual sodomy.*

However, B is neither a monster-barrer nor an exception-barrer. B is a Lakatosian lemma-incorporator. Logic dictates that a counterexample to the main proposition is also a counterexample to at least one lemma. Since homosexual sodomy is an apparent counterexample to the main proposition that there is a fundamental right to control the nature of one's intimate associations,

B must find the lemma that is also violated. Or does he? Doesn't B have the additional option of denying that this is a counterexample to the main proposition? B could say that homosexual sodomy is in fact one of the intimate associations over which individuals have a fundamental right to exercise control. In that case, no lemma would be violated. This is an option that is simply unavailable in mathematics. It is analogous to someone contending that the sum of the angles of any triangle on the surface of a sphere is in fact 180°.

The reason such arguments do not arise in mathematics is that mathematics, by definition, proceeds from assumed unprovable postulates. Modern mathematicians do not argue about whether Euclid's Fifth Postulate is true in some metaphysical sense. They know that some conjectures will be provable if that postulate is assumed true, and others will be provable if it is not. And that is about all there is to say in the realm of mathematics.

By contrast, legal arguments center around the truth or falsity of the preliminary assumptions. B will say to W: "I grant that if there is no right to homosexual sodomy, then my articulation of the fundamental right to control the nature of one's intimate associations is in fact too abstract. But the whole question is whether there is such a right to homosexual sodomy." As we concluded from our discussion of the relationship between law and literature, logical consistency is too weak a condition to discriminate between competing abstractions. Law is, ultimately, unlike mathematics.[35]

5

Reconstructing the Constitution as a Reader's Guide

CAN THE CONSTITUTION be made to channel value choice in a way that *eliminates* the levels of generality problem? In a 1989 Supreme Court case, Justice Scalia suggested that it can. His views seem so likely to be influential, and they so typify a jurisprudential style likely to have great appeal, that they merit close attention here. In *Michael H. v. Gerald D.,*[1] the Court upheld a California law denying parental rights to a man who claimed to be the biological father of a child born to a woman married to another man. In dissent, Justice Brennan argued that there is a fundamental liberty interest in the parent-child relationship.[2] Writing for himself and Chief Justice Rehnquist, Justice Scalia in footnote 6 dismissed Justice Brennan's choice of a level of abstraction as arbitrary:

> We do not understand why, having rejected our focus upon the societal tradition regarding the natural father's rights vis-à-vis a child whose mother is married to another man, Justice Brennan would choose to focus instead upon "parenthood." Why should the relevant category not be even more general—perhaps "family relationships"; or "personal relationships"; or even "emotional attachments in general"? Though the dissent has no basis for the level of generality it would select, we do: We refer to the most specific level at which a relevant tradition protecting, or denying protection to, the asserted right can be identified.[3]

Justice Scalia's footnote 6, which Justices O'Connor and Kennedy pointedly declined to join and which seems destined to take its place alongside Justice Stone's famous footnote 4 as one of

97

constitutional law's most provocative asides,[4] is both a recognition of the problem of abstraction and a claim to have solved it. In this chapter we argue that Justice Scalia's claim is false on several grounds: first, that the extraction of fundamental rights from societal traditions is no more value-neutral than is the extraction of fundamental rights from legal precedent; second, that there is no universal metric of specificity against which to measure an asserted right; and third, that even if Justice Scalia's program were workable, it would achieve a semblance of judicial neutrality only at the unacceptably high cost of near-complete abdication of the judicial responsibility to protect individual rights. Finally, after rejecting Justice Scalia's quest for value-neutrality, we return to the alternative value-laden approach to constitutional interpretation that we sketched in Chapters 2 and 3.

What Do Historical Traditions Prove?

We begin by noting that when Justice Scalia refers to a tradition, he means a historical tradition. Insofar as historical traditions are a source of values external to precedent, appeal to such traditions may provide the criteria for consistency that the precedents themselves do not provide. To use the chain-novel metaphor, historical traditions are to be the criteria of fit with what came before.

Justice Scalia is hardly the first to attempt to ground fundamental rights in historical tradition. Indeed, since justices generally do not merely assert but *argue* that they have expressed a fundamental right at the appropriate level of generality, they have looked to sources external to their own value systems, including history. Thus, for example, in *Moore v. City of East Cleveland,* the grandmother case discussed in Chapter 2, Justice Powell emphasized that the relevant constitutional inquiry should focus on whether an asserted liberty is "deeply rooted in this Nation's history and tradition."[5] On its face, looking at historical traditions seems perfectly—well, traditional.

What is novel about Justice Scalia's argument, however, is his implicit suggestion that historical traditions come equipped with instruction manuals explaining how abstractly they are to be described. Yet surely historical traditions are susceptible to even *greater* manipulation than are legal precedents. Were it not for

Justice Scalia's suggestion to the contrary, Justice Brennan would have been stating the obvious in observing that "reasonable people can disagree about the content of particular traditions."[6]

To acknowledge the manipulability of historical traditions is to recognize that all history is summary. The lens of the historical camera, in focusing on one event, necessarily blurs others. Take, for example, a question related to the clergy disqualification issue that we discussed in Chapter 1, but one that is still very much alive today: should the Establishment Clause of the First Amendment be understood to embody a deeply rooted tradition of separation of church and state, such that religious displays are barred from public property?[7] To what sources should we look for the guiding historical tradition?

Focusing on positive law, we would find that Massachusetts provided for local establishments as late as 1833.[8] Virginia, on the other hand, enacted "An Act for Establishing Religious Freedom" in 1786, before the United States Constitution was written. Written by Thomas Jefferson, the Act reflects his Enlightenment ideals.[9] At the level of positive law, then, there appears to be a conflicted tradition. But even if there were consensus among state legislatures, what would that prove? Does the emergence of minimum wage laws in the late nineteenth century indicate that previously there was an historical tradition recognizing a right to work for an arbitrarily small sum? That is how the *Lochner* Court, if it spoke the language of fundamental rights and historical traditions, might have viewed the matter. But another interpretation is available. The late emergence of minimum wage laws corresponded with increasing industrialization: what was formerly unnecessary became expedient. Prior to industrialization, legislators did not even think about the question of minimum wages, much less decide that they violated a fundamental right. Thus, the absence of positive laws encroaching upon a right does not indicate the fundamentality of that right.

Conversely, the presence of positive laws encroaching upon a right does not negate the fundamentality of that right. If it did, then governments would be free to violate constitutional norms by persisting in a pattern of unconstitutional enactments. However, as the Supreme Court has observed, "no one acquires a vested or protected right in violation of the Constitution by long use, even when that span of time covers our entire national existence and indeed predates it."[10]

Moreover, historical traditions, like rights themselves, exist at various levels of generality. Consider again the Virginia Act for Establishing Religious Freedom. Although Jefferson's text resonates with the ideals of the eighteenth-century European Enlightenment, historians have shown that the primary political impetus behind the Act's passage was not a spirit of enlightened ecumenicalism, but rather religious fervor. Nonconformist religious fundamentalists in Virginia—who, contrary to the Act's declaration otherwise, believed themselves infallible in ecclesiastical matters but lacked the numerical strength to establish their churches—decided that their own best hope for securing religious liberty lay with an alliance of convenience with the Jeffersonians.[11] Thus, at the level of positive law there may be an historical tradition of religious toleration in Virginia, but at the level of social attitudes the existence of such a tradition is subject to doubt.

Moreover, historians like William McLoughlin may well be correct that throughout the eighteenth and most of the nineteenth century the majority of Americans believed that religion and politics should mix in "the 'sweet harmony' of a Christian nation,"[12] thereby rejecting Jefferson's metaphorical wall of separation. Although this fact might be relevant to constitutional interpretation, it is hardly dispositive. Unless we are willing to say that the Constitution is whatever the majority practices—and to say this much is to reduce the Constitution to a dead letter—we should not rule out the possibility that Jefferson's "more consistent position[ ]" about the meaning of the Establishment Clause was right and his contemporary critics were wrong.[13] History provides ambiguous guidance both because historical traditions can be indeterminate, and because even when we discover a clear historical tradition it is hardly obvious what the existence of that tradition tells us about the Constitution's meaning.

It is clear that Justice Scalia is well aware of how difficult it is to distill a wide range of historical sources into a single judgment about what people thought about a particular institution or practice. He has conceded that originalist jurisprudence is very difficult to apply correctly because "the task requires the consideration of an enormous mass of material [and] immersing oneself in the political and intellectual atmosphere of the time—somehow placing out of mind knowledge that we have which an earlier age did not, and putting on beliefs, attitudes, philosophies, prejudices and loyalties that are not those of our day."[14] Justice Scalia has nonetheless gone on to say that he prefers the difficult originalist enterprise to subjective, and therefore illegitimate, nonoriginalist modes of constitutional interpretation.[15] In response to our contention that historical traditions are generally ambiguous, Justice Scalia might argue that it is better to admit some ambiguity than to abandon the historical enterprise entirely.

Whatever one thinks of this response, it completely fails to address the second weakness of the attempt to locate rights in historical traditions: how do we know when to reject a historical pattern or understanding? Justice Scalia notes that "even if it could be demonstrated unequivocally that [public flogging and hand-branding] were not cruel and unusual measures in 1791, [these practices] would not be sustained by our courts, and any espousal of originalism as a practical theory of exegesis must somehow come to terms with that reality."[16] Yet these remarks are applicable to *any* interpretive scheme that seeks to locate rights in the historical understanding of a prior age—to the quest for "the most specific level" no less than to originalism.

How Do We Measure Specificity?

We turn now to a second weakness in Justice Scalia's tradition-bound approach to constitutional interpretation. What precisely is the "most specific level at which a relevant tradition" exists? Are positive laws more or less specific than social attitudes? Are social attitudes about one subject, say gender, more or less specific than social attitudes about another, such as religion? To paraphrase Justice Scalia's trenchant observation in another context, this is akin to asking "whether a particular line is longer than a particular rock is heavy."[17]

The absence of a single dimension of specificity is a pervasive problem for the tradition-bound program. According to Justice Scalia, if "there were no societal tradition, either way, regarding the rights of the natural father of a child adulterously conceived, [the Court] would have to consult, and (if possible) reason from, the traditions regarding natural fathers in general."[18] As Justice Scalia states the problem, after traditions regarding the rights of the natural father of a child adulterously conceived, traditions regarding natural fathers in general are the next most specific. But why must this be so? Why not consult general traditions regarding children adulterously conceived, and reason from these? In other words, when we find that there is no relevant tradition concerning asserted right X under conditions 1 and 2, do we consult traditions concerning right X under condition 1 in general, or do we consult traditions concerning right X under condition 2 in general?

This is anything but a merely theoretical problem. In *Roe v. Wade,* for example, the Court argued that there was no long-standing tradition making abortion illegal.[19] In the parlance of Justice Scalia's tradition-bound approach, we might say that there is no dispositive tradition regarding the rights of a woman to control her reproductive freedom when that control means the destruction of a fetus. We would then have to look to the next most specific tradition. Is that next most specific tradition a tradition regarding women's reproductive freedom in general? Or is it a tradition regarding the rights of fetuses, as reflected in laws making feticide a crime when caused by someone other than the mother? If the former, then the Court would ask if the fundamental right to privacy includes the right not to reproduce. Since *Eisenstadt v. Baird*[20] answered that question affirmatively, the Court might reason from this tradition that there is a fundamental right to abortion. If the Court chooses traditions about feticide as the next most specific tradition, however, then it would have to hold that there is no fundamental right to abortion. Because Justice Scalia does not tell us how we are to measure the specificity of various traditions, he cannot escape the value-laden *choice* of a level, and a direction, of abstraction.

It might be objected that this difficulty arises only because we have concentrated on asserted rights about which there is no tradition exactly on point. After all, in *Michael H.* itself Justice Scalia claimed that he was able to avoid searching for a next most specific tradition because there was a specific tradition that "unqualifiedly denie[d] protection" to "the natural father of a child adulterously conceived."[21]

Even granting the existence of that "specific" tradition, however, this certainly is not a tradition that is *exactly* on point. We can imagine, for example, that there might be a tradition regarding people who had conducted adulterous affairs in a manner similar to this plaintiff in various detailed respects or, for that matter, a tradition regarding people resembling this father in other ways that many would deem "obviously" irrelevant—such as hair color, or race, or age. Of course we do not expect to find such ridiculous traditions because a basic principle of our legal system is that such a rule of law would be too specific, and therefore arbitrary. Yet, as was the case with the non-sequitur endings to *Great Expectations* that we encountered in Chapter 4, what counts as arbitrary is usually a matter of societal consensus rather than pure logic.

Justice Scalia's formulation of the rights at stake as the rights of "the natural father of a child adulterously conceived" is therefore already a considerable abstraction. He has abstracted away much information that virtually everybody would agree is irrelevant. But he has also abstracted away some information that many people would see as quite relevant. The natural father in *Michael H.* had a long-standing, albeit adulterous, relationship with the mother of his child. He also had fairly extensive contact with his child.[22] Surely this information is more significant than the plaintiff's race or age. A more specific formulation of the issue than Justice Scalia gives us would be: *What are the rights of the natural father of a child conceived in an adulterous but long-standing relationship, where the father has played a major role in the child's early development?*

It is unlikely that there is a tradition that addresses this very question at this precise level of specificity. Thus, we are left with the problem of specifying the *next* most specific tradition. Here, as in the abortion case, we find that there is no single dimension or direction along which to measure the degree of abstraction or generality. Do we abstract away the father's relationship with his child and her mother, as Justice Scalia does? Or do we instead abstract away the fact that the relationship with the mother was an adulterous one, as Justice Brennan does? If we do the latter, then we will find ourselves consulting traditions regarding natural fathers who play major roles in their children's development. This sounds very much like "traditions regarding natural fathers in general," which Justice Scalia regarded as less specific than his formulation of the problem. By starting from an even *more* specific description of the case than did Justice Scalia, we have seen that he had no greater justification for abstracting away the father-child relationship than Justice Brennan had for abstracting away the fact of adultery.

The Tradition-Bound Program in Practice

Justice Scalia is aware that his tradition-bound approach to constitutional interpretation would severely curtail the Supreme Court's role in protecting individual liberties. Indeed, since he regards judicial protection of unenumerated rights as illegitimate, such a curtailment would seem to be the purpose of his method. Thus, concurring in the 1990 case of *Cruzan v. Missouri Department of Health,*[23] Justice Scalia applied his *Michael H.* reasoning to conclude that "the federal courts have no business" pronouncing limits on state policies concerning the right to die.[24] As we noted in Chapter 2, a majority of the Court recognized an unenumerated constitutional right to die in that case. For Justice Scalia, this was anathema. He argued that "even when it is demonstrated by clear and convincing evidence that a patient no longer wishes certain measures to be taken to preserve her life, it is up to the citizens of Missouri to decide, through their elected representatives, whether that wish will be honored."[25]

Justice Scalia concluded his *Cruzan* concurrence by suggesting that his unwillingness "to create out of nothing" rights under the Due Process Clause would not leave individual rights unprotected against majority excesses. Instead, he suggested that liberty would be protected by a different route. Not the Due Process Clause, but the Equal Protection Clause, he wrote, "is the source of most of our protection," because it "requires the democratic majority to accept for themselves and their loved ones what they impose on you and me."[26] Thus, in a case like *Cruzan,* the democratic majority would be unlikely to formulate oppressive rules applicable to the terminally ill because they know that they may one day find themselves subject to those rules.

Perhaps Justice Scalia is correct when he suggests that the

citizenry does not need the Court's help in avoiding arbitrary impositions that harm everyone equally. Even if this is so—and if we recall Justice Powell's observation in the *Garcia* case that the Constitution protects the individual rights of those who have adequate representation no less than the rights of those who do not, it is not at all obvious why we should concede Justice Scalia's point[27]—it still does not follow that the Equal Protection Clause can protect *unpopular* liberties. Indeed, requiring that legislation apply to all citizens equally is a manifestly inadequate means of protecting many individual rights, as two simple illustrations will show.

Consider a statute banning homosexual sodomy. Such a law would apply to all citizens, heterosexual as well as homosexual, and so would impose the same constraint upon the democratic majority who enacted the law as it imposes on the minority who find that it curtails their liberty. Thus, under Justice Scalia's formulation, the law would be constitutional. The same would be true of a law banning flag-burning—which, by the way, is not mentioned in the literal text of the Constitution—since it would ban flag-burning by anyone.[28] In each of these cases the democratic majority proscribes an act that those in the majority have no intention of performing. Thus, such laws do not "impose" anything on the majority. These laws are impositions only for those in the minority who disagree with the policies that underlie them, for it is only their liberty that is in any meaningful sense curtailed.

Perhaps, then, Justice Scalia has in mind a notion of equal protection that focuses not so much upon the literal terms of a statute, but upon how it affects differently situated individuals. We might, for example, view a criminal homosexual sodomy statute as violating equal protection where the state does not also criminalize heterosexual vaginal intercourse. Similarly, we might view abortion prohibitions as denials of equal protection where the law does not also impose some analogous bodily burden upon men whenever conception occurs. However, to make such comparisons requires us to view the conduct proscribed at a fairly high level of generality. But at this point, the very same historical traditions that would lead Justice Scalia not to generalize for the purposes of the Due Process Clause would almost certainly prevent generalization under the Equal Protection Clause. As Justice Scalia apparently would use it, therefore, the Equal Protection Clause provides no greater protection for nontraditional liberties than does the Due Process Clause.[29]

The Potential Uses of a Tradition-Bound Interpretation

We have argued that the footnote 6 program is unworkable in two ways: that it merely shifts the problem of abstraction from the realm of legal precedent to that of historical precedent; and that it is ultimately incoherent because there is, in any event, no such thing as a "most specific level" of generality. As a theoretical matter, these problems seem inevitable given Justice Scalia's vain quest for a value-free constitutional touchstone, a quest symptomatic of (if more sophisticated than) the approach of many judicial conservatives.

The tradition-bound approach is therefore doomed to fail, at least on its own terms. Nevertheless, it might be argued that, even if there are *theoretical* difficulties with that approach, it is a valuable heuristic. Although it will not eliminate all aspects of judicial value choice, this argument would go, the tradition-bound method at least requires judges to make a serious effort to attempt to control for their own biases in specifying the level of generality of fundamental rights.

Although we agree that such an effort is vital, even this limited claim for the tradition-bound approach seems insupportable. Because it imports values surreptitiously—claiming all the while only to be discovering values that are, as it were, out there in societal traditions—it provides judges with a dangerous means to disguise, and thereby to distort, what is at stake. As Justice Brennan said of the doctrine of original intent, it is "arrogance cloaked as humility."[30]

To shed further light on how the tradition-bound methodology begs rather than addresses key constitutional questions, it will be useful to examine yet another of Justice Scalia's footnotes in *Michael H.*, footnote 4. Criticizing the Court's practice of first deciding whether a liberty is fundamental and then asking whether a particular government practice limiting that liberty can be justified, Justice Scalia stated for himself and three other members of the Court: "We cannot imagine what compels this strange procedure of looking at the act which is assertedly the subject of a liberty interest in isolation from its effect upon other people— rather like inquiring whether there is a liberty interest in firing a gun where the case at hand happens to involve its discharge into another person's body."[31]

One of us has recently written that this approach was virtually tailor-made as a means for overruling *Roe v. Wade*.[32] And indeed, it strongly echoes the position taken by Justice White, dissenting in *Thornburgh v. American College of Obstetricians and Gynecologists*.[33] But the *Michael H.* footnote 4 outlook has a far greater capacity: if faithfully carried out, it could eliminate *all* fundamental liberties. When the factors that provide the state's possible justifications for its regulation are automatically incorporated into the initial definition of a liberty, the fundamental nature of that liberty inevitably vanishes.

This is so because, unless the state's interest is absurd on its face, when it is suitably incorporated into an asserted liberty it will render that liberty so specific as to seem insupportable, or at least radically disconnected from precedent. The privacy right protected in *Roe* becomes the implausible "right" to destroy a living fetus; the free speech right protected in *New York Times Co. v. Sullivan*[34] becomes the dubious "right" to libel a public official; the right to an exclusionary remedy for Fourth Amendment violations protected in *Mapp v. Ohio*[35] becomes the counterintuitive "right" of a criminal to suppress the truth. To state these cases this way is to decide them in government's favor. Now it may well be that there are respectable arguments to be made that each of these cases was wrongly decided against the state. However, such arguments are *arguments* only if they purport to explain why the state interest outweighs the liberty interest. Under Justice Scalia's footnote 4 approach, by contrast, the state interest obliterates, without explanation and at the outset, any trace of the liberty at stake from the individual's perspective.

Nonetheless, Justice Scalia's footnote 4 can be read not as an end run around strict scrutiny for fundamental rights, but as a plea for greater judicial flexibility. After all, there really is something artificial in the two-step process that the Court deploys in its fundamental rights cases, asking first whether the asserted liberty is fundamental, and only then asking if it is outweighed by a compelling governmental interest. As Justice Stevens has observed in the equal protection context, the Supreme Court's "cases reflect a continuum of judgmental responses . . . which have been explained in opinions by terms ranging from 'strict scrutiny' at one extreme to 'rational basis' at the other [but] these so called 'standards' [do not] adequately explain the decisional process."[36]

Justice Stevens's point is that the degree to which a classification is suspect should vary with the purpose to which the classification is put. For instance, gender should not be a suspect classification when used for segregating public rest rooms, although it should be suspect when used as a basis for denying job opportunities. By analogy, Justice Scalia's footnote 4 in *Michael H.* might be taken merely as a call for allowing legislatures greater flexibility in responding to the wide range of human needs. Thus, it could be argued, the right to make procreative decisions is less fundamental when the decision involves external harms, such as the destruction of a fetus. It might be that all footnote 4 is meant to accomplish is the replacement of the bifurcated fundamental rights inquiry with a sliding scale that weighs the individual's liberty interest against the state interest. If so, then it is a relatively harmless suggestion.

However, there is nothing in Justice Scalia's *Michael H.* opinion, nor in his subsequent opinions applying this method, to suggest that he has in mind only the creation of a new balancing test. Indeed, given Justice Scalia's general hostility to balancing, this explanation seems quite dubious.[37]

The relationship of footnotes 4 and 6 in *Michael H.* illustrates the truly frightening potential of Justice Scalia's approach. Footnote 6 instructs us to look for the most specific tradition we can find with respect to an asserted liberty interest. Although (as we believe we have shown) the concept of a most specific tradition is incoherent, it is clear from footnote 4 that Justice Scalia means to have us start our search from a very specific liberty indeed— *one that has the state interest built into it from the start.* And it should also come as no surprise, as the examples we have just given illustrate, that the "liberty" to frustrate various state policies cannot count as a liberty that is deeply rooted in our traditions.

One can only conclude either that Justice Scalia's method is designed to overrule virtually all of the Court's decisions protecting individual rights—a rather unlikely supposition—or, more likely, that it is a construct to be deployed selectively, allowing judges to define rights more or less abstractly depending upon their own views of how important those rights are, or of how they score on some other index every bit as extra-constitutional as the one that Justice Scalia accuses Justice Brennan of deploying. What Justice Scalia heralds as a means for assuring greater judicial objectivity turns out to be quite the opposite.

The Virtue of Consistency

In our efforts to avoid the fallacy of hyper-integration we would do well to heed the warning of Justice Cardozo, who noted that a legal principle, once enunciated, will tend to expand to its logical limit, occupying fields for which it was not crafted.[38] The danger he perceived was that, in striving for a coherent and consistent body of law, we might so exalt abstract principles that we would lose sight of our commonsense notions about justice. But there is also virtue in consistency. To the extent that a mode of thought exists that may be identified as "legal," it has everything to do with evenhandedly applying general principles to concrete situations. A prerequisite for the lawyer's art, therefore, is the enunciation of principles. A principle is distinguished from an intuition by the fact that a principle is abstract; it connects our intuitions about specific fact situations at a higher level of abstraction. This is the method of the common law.

The call for more abstract principles regarding the contours and contents of protected realms of liberty and equality, although dangerous in the way that Justice Cardozo warned, is on the whole a source of progressive pressure. For our abstractions push us constantly to check our practices against our principles. Consider, for example, the promise contained in the Declaration of Independence that "all men are created equal." A philosophy that refused to generalize would attempt to confine this declaration: by "all men" the Continental Congress meant only propertied men, or only free men, or only white men, or only men who simultaneously belong to all three of those categories. Each of these statements may be partly correct as a matter of historical truth, but we would argue, as have Ronald Dworkin and others, that it is the *principle* of equality, the *abstraction* of equality, that became our constitutional legacy from our Revolutionary and, most significantly, our Civil War forebears.[39] The nation in which equality existed *only* as an abstraction was a nation, quite literally, at war with itself. The nation we are *becoming* may, we hope, be one in which equality is both generalized and concretized.

Perhaps in a perfect world, the generalization of rights would be accomplished by elected legislatures. But recall the words of James Madison with which we began Chapter 1: men are not angels. The Framers of our Constitution understood that this is not a perfect world, and thus, like it or not, judges must squarely face the task of deciding how to define our liberties abstractly. The requirement that fundamental rights be connected to the constitutional text in the way we sketched in Chapter 2 provides one check on the tendency of judges to choose a level of abstraction to suit their own subjective preferences. This provides a partial response to the charge that "[t]here is no apparent reason why the Court should manipulate the level of generality to protect unconventional sexual behavior any more than liberty should be taken at a high enough level of abstraction to protect kleptomania."[40] The Constitution's repeated references to "property" seem pretty squarely to foreclose any argument that there is a fundamental right for one person to deprive another of her property.

By contrast, nothing in the Constitution's text remotely forecloses the argument that unconventional sexual behavior is a fundamental right. If we are to take seriously the Ninth Amendment's requirement that "[t]he enumeration in the Constitution, of certain rights, shall not be construed to deny or disparage others retained by the people," at a minimum we must consider the possibility that rights which are *consistent* with the enumerated rights—as a right to choose unconventional sexual behavior is, and as a "right" to engage in theft surely is not—may be *required* by the Constitution.

The Ninth Amendment tells judges, legislators, and other interpreters of the Constitution how *not* to "construe" that document. We would argue that to make sense of the Ninth

Amendment's *proscriptive* role requires readers of the Constitution to assume that it also plays a *prescriptive* role. What the Ninth Amendment counsels against is the portrayal of the enumerated rights as isolated islands of special protection, elevated above the surrounding sea of possible unenumerated rights "retained by the people," for to elevate the enumerated rights in this way would surely "disparage" those that remain submerged. If the Ninth Amendment condemns such a *dis-integrated* vision, then it must condone the opposite vision elaborated by Justice Harlan in his *Poe v. Ullman* dissent. The Ninth Amendment thereby affirmatively acts as a presumption in favor of generalizing.

In addition to the requirement of consistency with the assumptions underlying the constitutional text, other checks on result-orientation in the selection of a level of generality are also available. In an earlier work, one of us suggested that the test should be whether the asserted level of generality provides an appropriate description of already-protected rights without reference to the newly-asserted rights. Judges should ask whether the abstraction is a bona fide tradition or "a mere concoction for litigational purposes."[41] First, the Court must determine what concerns actually underlay the prior decisions; only after the Court has selected the appropriate level of abstraction at which to describe those concerns should it test the asserted specific right against that abstraction. Such a prescription is hardly radical: the dissent in *Michael H.* proceeds much along these lines, first arguing that the prior cases support a right to parenthood that is broader than the "unitary family," and only then locating the specific right within the general description.[42]

Again, this program does not *eliminate* judicial value-choice, but it does channel it considerably. It does so by requiring that, in characterizing its prior cases, the Court look not only to what those cases held, but also to the essential reasons for those holdings. To borrow from Lakatos's model of mathematical proof discussed in Chapter 4, judges should be lemma-incorporators. Just as a mathematical lemma-incorporator preserves not only the proposition but also its proof, so a judicial lemma-incorporator should preserve not only the holding of a prior case but also its rationale. An abstraction that has been concocted merely for litigational purposes will often be recognizable as such because it is consistent only with the holdings of prior cases, not with their rationales.

Essential Attributes and Judicial Nihilism

The anti-generalizing approach exemplified by footnote 6 of *Michael H.* is perhaps best described as a form of judicial nihilism. It denies that there are *essential* aspects to prior cases. By suggesting that only specific historical traditions can fix the appropriate level of generality at which to define rights, Justice Scalia implicitly assumes that there is no way to read the prior cases on their own terms so as to discern rationally the level of generality at which a right was recognized. This assumption by Justice Scalia is impossible to square with much of what we ordinarily think the judicial enterprise entails.

To see the nihilistic nature of the premises underlying Justice Scalia's tradition-bound method of interpretation, consider a hypothetical question that a law professor might have posed to her students before the decision in *Roe v. Wade:* would the contraception case, *Griswold v. Connecticut,*[43] have come out the other way if it had involved a so-called abortion pill—that is, if it had concerned not the right to have sex without conception occurring, but the right to have sex without bearing a child notwithstanding the fact that conception did occur? The purpose of the law professor's question would be to test the limits of the Court's reasoning. Ordinarily, we would expect that in the ensuing discussion students would marshal various arguments explaining why the fact that conception had not yet occurred in *Griswold* was or was not essential to the case.

Those students who believed that the timing of the decision not to bear a child was essential to *Griswold* could point to the majority's references to the inviolability of the home through its invocation of the Third and Fourth Amendments, and its rhetorical question: "Would we allow the police to search the sacred precincts of marital bedrooms for telltale signs of the use of contraceptives?"[44] Thus, they could argue, critical to *Griswold* is the fact that the Connecticut ban on contraceptive use applied to an activity that takes place in the home. They might then draw a line that distinguishes between an abortion performed in the public setting of a hospital or other medical facility, and one accomplished by the ingestion of a pill in the privacy of one's home.

The students who believed that a right broad enough to include all forms of abortion was essential to *Griswold* would argue that the principal focus of the *Griswold* opinion was the marriage relationship. They would note that a state prohibition on abortions would have no less "destructive impact"[45] upon the relationship of a husband and wife who wished to obtain an abortion in a hospital than the Connecticut law had upon the relationship of a husband and wife who wished to use contraceptives in their home.

As in most law school discussions, there may be no "correct" answer to this hard case. If we attempt to place each fact of *Griswold* on one of two lists, one containing essential facts and the other containing nonessential facts, we will find that reasonable people will disagree over where some facts belong. However, there will be widespread agreement concerning many others. For instance, nearly everyone would agree that the race of the Griswolds belongs on the nonessential list, while the fact that the case involves an intimate act belongs on the essential list. As with so many legal questions, the interesting argument over what constitutes an essential fact will concern how and where to draw lines.

Now imagine how the discussion would differ in a law school in which Justice Scalia's tradition-bound approach prevails. With each fact we change we must search in vain for a historical tradition regarding the new case that results. Thus, it is impossible to discuss how a case differs when one fact is changed. In the world of tradition-bound interpretation, we cannot say how *Griswold* would have differed if it had involved the right to bear a child notwithstanding the fact that conception has occurred, any more than we can say how *Griswold* would have differed if it had involved an entirely different subject, such as the right to drive without a seat belt.

Yet surely there is a qualitative difference between these two variations on the facts of *Griswold*. In the former example we have abstracted away a fact that may or may not be important, and our discussion will focus on whether that fact should be deemed important. But in the latter example we have abstracted away the whole case. Had *Griswold* involved the right to use an abortion pill, it might have come out differently, but if it had involved the right to drive without a seat belt it would not even have been *Griswold*. It would have been some other case.

Of course the anti-generalizer could respond that *Griswold* would be a different case if we changed any fact at all. If we were philosophers of language, this response might spark an interesting debate. Some philosophers have taken the position that there is nothing essential to an object beyond some list of properties that we *define* as essential to it.[46] Others, like Saul Kripke, have criticized this view, noting that people ordinarily speak as if there is a difference between necessary and contingent properties of various objects or persons.[47] For instance, although we may have a difficult time formulating complete lists of the essential and non-essential properties of Richard Nixon (or "Nixonhood"), we can make a pretty good guess as to how to classify many of his properties. Because we can make sense of the question, "What would the world have been like if Nixon had lost the 1968 presidential election?" we can say that "winning in 1968" is not an essential property of Nixonhood. By contrast, a question like, "What if Nixon were a moose?" is meaningless because it is impossible for us to conceive of Nixon as being a moose and yet still being Nixon. "Being a human being," or at least "not being a moose," is an *essential* property of Nixonhood.[48]

There may well be *philosophical* objections to a theory of essential properties that proceeds along the lines of these examples. As a *practical* matter, however, law must proceed from the assumption that judges can tell the difference between the essential and the trivial in reading and applying prior decisions. Otherwise, there would be no such thing as precedent, and indeed no such thing as law.

The Method of the Common Law

We have argued that judges possess the requisite tools to make principled distinctions in the selection of a level of generality in defining fundamental rights. Among other things, a too-abstract right will be recognizable as such whenever its enunciation requires us to ignore much of what was said in the cases that allegedly established it. Thus, for example, someone who attempted to extend the privacy cases to include the specific right of one consenting adult to sell narcotic drugs to another, based upon a general right of consenting adults "to do whatever they please so long as they injure no innocent bystanders," would have to ignore much of the language in those cases making clear that only *certain* decisions are fundamentally private in character because "*a certain* private sphere of individual liberty will be kept largely beyond the reach of government."[49] The clear implication of this language is that some aspects of liberty are not fundamental. Just as the Constitution's repeated references to private property render fatuous any asserted right to steal, so the concern for the preservation of human life expressed in both the Fifth and Fourteenth Amendments undercuts a fundamental liberty interest in assisting an otherwise healthy individual to poison herself.

No doubt the boundaries of the "certain private sphere" are difficult to ascertain, and are fluid through time.[50] Yet to marshal this uncertainty in support of a jurisprudence that allows traditions of intolerance to insulate intrusive government activities forever from constitutional scrutiny is to question much more than the enterprise of fundamental rights: it is to question law itself. Charles Black's critique of those who would read the Ninth Amendment out of the Constitution seems particularly appropriate here. Black noted that "a corpus juris of human rights . . . will never be built; it will always be building, like the common law. If this method [of generalizing rights] is not rational, then neither is the common law. And neither is any other attempt to give due effect to similarities and differences between already decided and newly presented cases and problems."[51]

Nonetheless, perhaps fearing accusations that their reading of the Constitution has no firmer basis than the pre-1937 reading that exalted economic rights, even progressive scholars increasingly hesitate to generalize fundamental rights. Thus, in an interesting effort to contain the *Hardwick* majority's effort to define rights narrowly and "conservatively," Cass Sunstein of the University of Chicago has advanced an argument to the effect that one might reconcile an anti-generalizing, tradition-conserving approach to "liberty" with a more capacious and tradition-shattering approach to "equal protection."[52]

There is one rather large textual problem with this theory. The

Constitution contains no Equal Protection Clause applicable to the federal government; the Fourteenth Amendment applies only to the states. That is why, when the Supreme Court ruled in *Bolling v. Sharpe* that federally operated segregated schools in the District of Columbia were unconstitutional, it relied on the Due Process Clause of the Fifth Amendment, which does apply to the federal government.[53] That decision, handed down the same day as *Brown v. Board of Education*,[54] is extremely problematic for originalists, since it cannot seriously be maintained that the Framers of the Fifth Amendment in 1789, many of whom owned slaves, intended to invalidate segregated schools—or even to embrace a norm of equality. But *Bolling v. Sharpe* is also problematic for Sunstein's theory, since it held, in a quite tradition-shattering manner, that segregating African-American schoolchildren "constitutes an arbitrary deprivation of their liberty."[55] The case seems radically inconsistent with Sunstein's tradition-conserving approach to "liberty."

If we could overlook this difficulty, we might be inclined to agree that as a matter of advocacy and legal strategy, Sunstein's proposal is a good one. As a matter of constitutional theory, however, his approach seems somewhat dubious. It is hard to imagine a defensible approach to the two clauses that does not take greater account of the inseparability of liberty and equality.

The basic choice to be made—and it is a choice that neither the Constitution's text nor its structure nor its history can make for us—is a choice between emphasizing the "conservative" functions of both the liberty and equality clauses (as well as others), and emphasizing their potential as generators of critique and change. The choice one makes must be justified extra-textually but may and should then be implemented in ways that draw as much guidance as possible from the text itself.

Justice Harlan exemplified such a program in his *Poe* dissent, in which he opted for a moderately conservative orientation toward generalization—one considerably less tradition-conserving than Justice Scalia's, however—and proceeded to seek unifying structures for specified rights in an intermediate level of generality drawing heavily upon textual points of reference.

In this spirit, as we noted in our discussion of *Hardwick* in Chapter 2, if one is willing to generalize much at all, the Constitution's text—in the First Amendment's protection of peaceful assembly and in the special solicitude for the home in the Third Amendment and the Fourth Amendment—points toward generalizing in the direction of intimate personal association in the privacy of the home rather than generalizing in the direction of, let us say, freedom of choice in matters of procreation.

It is for this reason that *Hardwick* seems to us so egregiously wrong; that *Roe* seems a closer and more difficult case; that a supposed "fundamental right" to use a sperm bank would represent a particularly bold leap; and that a "right" to enforce a surrogacy contract against a woman who has changed her mind and wishes to keep her gestational child would seem to entail a leap across a constitutionally unbridgeable void. Indeed, it would entail a leap beyond anything we could comfortably describe as *reading* the Constitution. And it is the process of reading the Constitution that this book has sought to illuminate.

Notes

Index

Notes

Introduction

1. John Paul Stevens, "Judicial Restraint," *San Diego Law Review*, 22 (May-June 1985), 437.

2. Michael Kammen, *A Machine That Would Go of Itself: The Constitution in American Culture* (New York: Knopf, 1986), p. 3.

3. *Texas v. Johnson*, 109 S. Ct. 2533 (1989); *United States v. Eichman*, 110 S. Ct. 2404 (1990).

4. "Constitutional Amendment to Bar Flag Burning Fails in House," *New York Times*, June 22, 1990, p. A14, col. 5. See also "Senate Rejects New Move to Outlaw Flag Burning," *New York Times*, June 27, 1990, p. B6, col. 4.

5. *Ohio v. Akron Center for Reproductive Health*, 110 S. Ct. 2972 (1990); *Hodgson v. Minnesota*, 110 S. Ct. 2926 (1990).

6. *Cruzan v. Missouri Department of Health*, 110 S. Ct. 2841 (1990).

7. Linda Greenhouse, "A Divided Supreme Court Ends the Term with a Bang," *New York Times*, July 1, 1990, p. E3.

8. See Robert Bork, *The Tempting of America* (New York: The Free Press, 1989), pp. 281–293.

9. See Ethan Bronner, *Battle for Justice: How the Bork Nomination Shook America* (New York: W. W. Norton, 1989).

10. *Abington School Dist. v. Schempp*, 374 U.S. 203 (1963), and *Engel v. Vitale*, 370 U.S. 421 (1962) (school prayer); *Roe v. Wade*, 410 U.S. 113 (1973) (abortion). On the Court's reaffirmation, see *Wallace v. Jaffree*, 472 U.S. 38 (1985) (school prayer); *Thornburgh v. American College of Obstetricians and Gynecologists*, 476 U.S. 747 (1986), and *Akron v. Akron Center for Reproductive Health, Inc.*, 462 U.S. 416 (1983) (abortion).

11. See *Webster v. Reproductive Health Services*, 109 S. Ct. 3040 (1989); *Ohio* and *Minnesota* cases (abortion); *Richmond v. J. A. Croson Co.*, 109 S. Ct. 706 (1989) (affirmative action).

12. See Laurence Tribe, *American Constitutional Law,* 2nd ed. (Mineola, N.Y.: Foundation Press, 1988), § 8-6, p. 580.

13. Ibid., § 13-7, p. 1074, and § 13-8, p. 1076 (reapportionment); § 16-18, p. 1488 (desegregation).

1. How Not to Read the Constitution

1. James Madison, "The Federalist No. 51," *The Federalist Papers* (New York: Random House, 1937), p. 337.

2. See "Letter from Thomas Jefferson to James Madison," Paris, March 15, 1789, in Adrienne Koch and William Peden, *The Life and Selected Writings of Thomas Jefferson* (New York: Modern Library, 1972), p. 462; Adrienne Koch, *Jefferson and Madison: The Great Collaboration* (New York: Oxford University Press, 1964), p. 58.

3. Thomas Grey, "The Constitution as Scripture," *Stanford Law Review,* 37 (November 1984), 1; Sanford Levinson, "'The Constitution' in American Civil Religion," *Supreme Court Review,* 1979 (1979), 123; Robert A. Burt, "Constitutional Law and the Teaching of the Parables," *Yale Law Journal,* 93 (January 1984), 455; Robert M. Cover, "Foreword—The Supreme Court, 1982 Term: 'Nomos' and Narrative," *Harvard Law Review,* 97 (November 1983), 4.

4. James White, *When Words Lose Their Meaning: Constitutions and Reconstitutions of Language, Character, and Community* (Chicago: University of Chicago Press, 1984), pp. 231–247.

5. Michael Kammen, *A Machine That Would Go of Itself: The Constitution in American Culture* (New York: Knopf, 1986), p. 125 (emphasis added).

6. 252 U.S. 416 (1920).

7. Ibid., p. 433 (emphasis added).

8. Ibid., pp. 433–434.

9. Gary Wills, *Inventing America: Jefferson's Declaration of Independence* (New York: Doubleday, 1978), pp. xxiv–xxvi.

10. Raoul Berger, *Government by Judiciary: The Transformation of the Fourteenth Amendment* (Cambridge, Mass.: Harvard University Press, 1977), p. 7.

11. E.g., Edwin Meese, "Toward a Jurisprudence of Original Intention," *Benchmark,* 2 (January-February 1986), 1.

12. See *The Constitution of the United States of America: Analysis and Interpretation,* S. Doc. 92-82, 92nd Cong., 2d sess. (1972), p. 31 n.6.

13. Berger, *Government by Judiciary,* pp. 10–19.

14. See *United States v. Miller,* 307 U.S. 174 (1939).

15. Sanford Levinson, "The Embarrassing Second Amendment," *Yale Law Journal,* 99 (December 1989), 637.

16. Paul Brest, "The Misconceived Quest for the Original Understanding," *Boston University Law Review*, 60 (1980), 204.

17. Ibid., p. 234.

18. *McDaniel v. Paty*, 435 U.S. 618, 637 (1978). See Laurence Tribe, *American Constitutional Law*, 2nd ed. (Mineola, N.Y.: Foundation Press, 1988), § 14-8.

19. *Brown v. Board of Education*, 347 U.S. 483, 492–493 (1954).

20. See Ronald Dworkin, *Law's Empire* (Cambridge, Mass.: Harvard University Press, 1986), pp. 387–389. See also Tribe, *American Constitutional Law*, § 16-15, pp. 1477–78; § 16-21, p. 1514.

21. William Rehnquist, "The Notion of a Living Constitution," *Texas Law Review*, 54 (May 1976), 693, 694.

22. *Thornburgh v. American College of Obstetricians*, 476 U.S. 747, 789 (1986) (White, J., dissenting).

23. Kammen, *A Machine That Would Go of Itself*, p. 1.

24. Laurence Tribe, *Constitutional Choices* (Cambridge, Mass.: Harvard University Press, 1985).

25. Richard Posner, "Book Review," *Michigan Law Review*, 84 (February-April 1986), 551.

26. Richard Posner, "What Am I? A Potted Plant?" *New Republic*, September 28, 1987, p. 23.

27. Posner, "Book Review," p. 551.

28. See Richard Posner, "The DeFunis Case and the Preferential Treatment of Minorities," *Supreme Court Review*, 1974 (1974), 1, 25; Tribe, *American Constitutional Law*, § 16-22, p. 1526.

29. Kammen, *A Machine That Would Go of Itself*, p. 1.

30. Dworkin, *Law's Empire*, pp. 379–389.

31. Grey, "The Constitution as Scripture," p. 19.

32. See, e.g., Michael Perry, *The Constitution, the Courts, and Human Rights: An Inquiry into the Legitimacy of Constitutional Policymaking by the Judiciary* (New Haven, Conn.: Yale University Press, 1982).

33. Henry Monaghan, "Our Perfect Constitution," *New York University Law Review*, 56 (May-June 1981), 353.

34. John Paul Stevens, "Judicial Restraint," *San Diego Law Review*, 22 (May-June 1985), 437.

35. See Hilary Putnam, *Reason, Truth, and History* (Cambridge: Cambridge University Press, 1981); Frank I. Michelman, "Justification (and Justifiability) of Law in a Contradictory World," in *NOMOS: Justification*, vol. 28, ed. J. Roland Pennock and John Chapman (New York: New York University Press, 1986). See the discussion of nihilism in Friedrich Nietzsche, *The Will to Power*, trans. A. Ludovic (New York: Russell and Russell, 1964).

36. See Bruce A. Ackerman, "The Storrs Lectures: Discovering the Constitution," *Yale Law Journal,* 93 (May 1984), 1013.

37. See William J. Brennan, "Constitutional Adjudication and the Death Penalty: A View from the Court," *Harvard Law Review,* 100 (December 1986), 313, 323–331.

38. See Mark V. Tushnet, "Book Review," *Michigan Law Review,* 78 (March 1980), 694, 696–702.

39. Amends. 5 and 14, § 1 (due process), amend. 5 (private property).

40. See Tribe, *American Constitutional Law,* § 9–7, pp. 607–608.

41. See *National League of Cities v. Usery,* 426 U.S. 833, 856 (1976) (Brennan, J., joined by White and Marshall, JJ., dissenting).

42. Art. I, § 3, cl. 1.

43. See *Garcia v. San Antonio Metropolitan Transit Authority,* 469 U.S. 528, 554 (1985).

44. See Derrick Bell, "The Supreme Court, 1984 Term—Foreword: The Civil Rights Chronicles," *Harvard Law Review,* 99 (November 1985), 4–7, 7 n.9. See generally Thurgood Marshall, "Commentary: Reflections on the Bicentennial of the United States Constitution," *Harvard Law Review,* 101 (November 1987), 1.

45. See Ackerman, "The Storrs Lectures."

46. See Laurence Tribe, "A *Constitution* We Are Amending: In Defense of a Restrained Judicial Role," *Harvard Law Review,* 97 (December 1983), 433, 438–443.

47. Walter F. Murphy, "An Ordering of Constitutional Values," *Southern California Law Review,* 53 (1980), 703, 755–756.

48. 110 S. Ct. 2404, 2407 (1990). See also *Texas v. Johnson,* 109 S. Ct. 2533 (1989).

49. 109 S. Ct. at 2543 (citing *Boos v. Barry,* 108 S. Ct. 1157 (1988), and *Frisby v. Schultz,* 108 S. Ct. 2495 (1988)).

50. John Hart Ely, *Democracy and Distrust: A Theory of Judicial Review* (Cambridge, Mass.: Harvard University Press, 1980).

51. Amend. XIV, § 1.

52. John Hart Ely, "The Wages of Crying Wolf: A Comment on *Roe v. Wade,*" *Yale Law Journal,* 82 (April 1973), 920, 949.

53. Jesse Choper, *Judicial Review and the National Political Process: A Functional Reconsideration of the Role of the Supreme Court* (Chicago: University of Chicago Press, 1980).

54. *Immigration and Naturalization Serv. v. Chadha,* 462 U.S. 919 (1983).

55. *Bowsher v. Synar,* 478 U.S. 714 (1986).

56. Richard Epstein, *Takings: Private Property and the Power of Eminent Domain* (Cambridge, Mass.: Harvard University Press, 1985).

57. Thomas C. Grey, "The Malthusian Constitution," *University of Miami Law Review,* 41 (November 1986), 21, 22.

58. Epstein, *Takings,* pp. 200–201.
59. David Richards, *Toleration and the Constitution* (New York: Oxford University Press, 1986).
60. David Richards, "Interpretation and Historiography," *Southern California Law Review,* 58 (January 1985), 489, 542.
61. See, e.g., Mark Tushnet, "The Dilemmas of Liberal Constitutionalism," *Ohio State Law Journal,* 42 (1981), 411.
62. See generally Paul Brest, "The Fundamental Rights Controversy: The Essential Contradictions of Normative Constitutional Scholarship," *Yale Law Journal,* 90 (April 1981), 1063.
63. See Tribe, *American Constitutional Law,* p. 12 n.6.
64. See, e.g., Robert F. Nagel and Jack H. Nagel, "Theory of Choice," *New Republic,* July 23, 1990, p. 16.
65. Walt Whitman, "Song of Myself," *Leaves of Grass,* 9th ed. (1891–92), lines 1324–26.

2. Structuring Constitutional Conversations

1. We are grateful to Robert Fisher and Barack Obama for the metaphor of constitutional interpretation as conversation.
2. *City of London v. Wood,* 88 Eng. Rep. 1592, 1602 (1700).
3. William Van Alstyne, "Interpreting *This* Constitution: The Unhelpful Contributions of Special Theories of Judicial Review," *University of Florida Law Review,* 35 (1983), 209, 209–210.
4. *Dred Scott v. Sanford,* 60 U.S. (19 How.) 393 (1857).
5. Michael Kammen, *A Machine That Would Go of Itself: The Constitution in American Culture* (New York: Knopf, 1986), p. 125.
6. Art. I, § 9, cl. 3.
7. *Nixon v. Administrator of General Services,* 433 U.S. 425, 468–484 (1977).
8. Ibid., p. 472.
9. Ibid., pp. 536–545 (Burger, C. J., dissenting).
10. *People ex rel. Arcara v. Cloud Books, Inc.,* 65 N.Y.2d 324, 491 N.Y.S.2d 307, 480 N.E.2d 1089 (1985).
11. *Arcara v. Cloud Books, Inc.,* 478 U.S. 697, 708–713 (1986) (Blackmun, J., joined by Brennan and Marshall, JJ., dissenting).
12. *Bowsher v. Synar,* 478 U.S. 714 (1986).
13. 478 U.S., p. 708 (O'Connor, J., concurring).
14. Ibid.
15. Ibid., p. 3179.
16. *Texas v. Johnson,* 109 S. Ct. 2533, 2548 (1989) (Kennedy, J., concurring).
17. Art. I, § 8, cl. 3.

18. See Laurence Tribe, *American Constitutional Law,* 2nd ed. (Mineola, N.Y.: Foundation Press, 1988), §§ 5-4 to 5-6.

19. *Community Communications Co. v. City of Boulder,* 455 U.S. 40 (1982).

20. *Parker v. Brown,* 317 U.S. 341 (1943).

21. *Fisher v. City of Berkeley,* 475 U.S. 260 (1986).

22. *Heart of Atlanta Motel Inc. v. United States,* 379 U.S. 241, 258–259 (1964).

23. See *Hans v. Louisiana,* 134 U.S. 1 (1890); *Pennhurst State School & Hospital v. Halderman,* 465 U.S. 89 (1984).

24. See Tribe, *American Constitutional Law,* §§ 3-25 to 3-27.

25. See, e.g., Martha Field, "Comment: *Garcia v. San Antonio Metropolitan Transit Authority:* The Demise of a Misguided Doctrine," *Harvard Law Review,* 99 (November 1985), 84.

26. 426 U.S. 833 (1976).

27. Ibid., pp. 842–843.

28. *Garcia v. San Antonio Metropolitan Transit Authority,* 469 U.S. 528 (1985).

29. Ibid., pp. 564–567 and n.8 (Powell, J., joined by Burger, C.J., and Rehnquist and O'Connor, JJ., dissenting).

30. Charles Black, *Structure and Relationship in Constitutional Law* (Baton Rouge: Louisiana State University Press, 1969).

31. 440 U.S. 410 (1979).

32. Ibid., p. 433 (Rehnquist, J., joined by Burger, C.J., dissenting).

33. See Stanley Fish, *Is There a Text in This Class? The Authority of Interpretive Communities* (Cambridge, Mass.: Harvard University Press, 1980).

34. 456 U.S. 742, 789 (1982) (O'Connor, J., joined by Burger, C.J., and Rehnquist, J., concurring in the judgment in part and dissenting in part).

35. Ibid.

36. See *Luther v. Borden,* 48 U.S. (7 How.) 1 (1849); Tribe, *American Constitutional Law,* § 3-13, pp. 98–99.

37. 478 U.S. 109 (1986).

38. See Tribe, *American Constitutional Law,* § 5-23.

39. Ibid.

40. 472 U.S. 38 (1985).

41. Ibid., pp. 91–114 (Rehnquist, J., dissenting).

42. Ibid., pp. 67–84 (O'Connor, J., concurring in the judgment).

43. See William Rehnquist, "The Notion of a Living Constitution," *Texas Law Review,* 54 (May 1976), 693, 694.

44. *County of Allegheny v. ACLU,* 109 S. Ct. 3086, 3121 (1989) (O'Connor, J., concurring in part and concurring in the judgment).

45. See Tribe, *American Constitutional Law,* § 14-3, p. 1163 n.40.

46. Ibid., § 12-2.

47. 430 U.S. 705 (1977).

48. 413 U.S. 528 (1973).

49. 477 U.S. 635 (1986).

50. Ibid., pp. 643–647 (Marshall, J., dissenting).

51. *Meyer v. Nebraska,* 262 U.S. 390 (1923).

52. *Pierce v. Society of Sisters,* 268 U.S. 510 (1925); *Pierce v. Hill Military Academy,* 268 U.S. 510 (1925).

53. *Skinner v. Oklahoma,* 316 U.S. 535 (1942).

54. 381 U.S. 479 (1965).

55. 388 U.S. 1 (1967).

56. 405 U.S. 438 (1972).

57. 410 U.S. 113 (1973).

58. 431 U.S. 494 (1977).

59. See *Webster v. Reproductive Health Services,* 109 S. Ct. 3040 (1989). See also *Cruzan v. Missouri Department of Health,* 110 S. Ct. 2841, 2851 n.7 (1990).

60. *Nevada v. Hall,* 440 U.S. 410, 433 (1979) (Rehnquist, J., joined by Burger, C.J., dissenting).

61. Robert Bork, *The Tempting of America* (New York: The Free Press, 1989), p. 49.

62. *Turner v. Safley,* 107 S. Ct. 2254, 2265 (1987).

63. *Washington v. Harper,* 110 S. Ct. 1028, 1037 (1990).

64. 110 S. Ct. 2841.

65. 110 S. Ct. p. 2856 n.12.

66. Ibid., pp. 2856–57 (O'Connor, J., concurring).

67. Ibid., p. 2863 (Scalia, J., concurring).

68. 83 U.S. (16 Wall.) 36 (1873).

69. Art. IV, § 2, cl. 1.

70. See Tribe, *American Constitutional Law,* § 7-2, pp. 548–553.

71. Bork, *The Tempting of America,* p. 166.

72. See Lon Fuller, *The Morality of Law,* 2nd ed. (New Haven, Conn.: Yale University Press, 1969), pp. 81–91.

73. See, e.g., *Richmond Newspapers, Inc. v. Virginia,* 448 U.S. 555, 579–580 and n.15 (1980) (plurality opinion of Burger, C.J.); John Hart Ely, *Democracy and Distrust: A Theory of Judicial Review* (Cambridge, Mass.: Harvard University Press, 1980), pp. 34–41; Norman Redlich, "Are There 'Certain Rights . . . Retained by the People'?" *New York University Law Review,* 37 (November 1962), 787, 810–812.

74. *Griswold v. Connecticut,* 381 U.S. 479, 486–493 (1965) (Goldberg, J., joined by Warren, C.J., and Brennan, J., concurring).

75. *Richmond Newspapers, Inc. v. Virginia,* 448 U.S. 555 (1980).
76. Ibid., pp. 579–580 (plurality opinion of Burger, C.J., joined by White and Stevens, JJ.).
77. 478 U.S. 186 (1986).
78. Transcript of the Hearings before the Senate Judiciary Comm. on the Nomination of William H. Rehnquist to be Chief Justice of the United States, July 30, 1986, pp. 181–183.
79. Ibid., p. 183.
80. "Mr. Power: Attorney General Edwin Meese," *New York Times,* October 12, 1986, § 6, pp. 18, 92.
81. *Thornburgh v. American College of Obstetricians and Gynecologists,* 476 U.S. 747 (1986).
82. Ibid., pp. 788–794 (White, J., joined by Rehnquist, J., dissenting); *Hardwick,* 478 U.S., pp. 191–196.
83. "Transcript of Oral Arguments before Court on Abortion Case," *New York Times,* April 27, 1989, p. B12.
84. *Webster,* 109 S. Ct., p. 3057 (plurality opinion).
85. Ibid.
86. J. A. Simpson and E. S. C. Weiner, eds., *The Oxford English Dictionary,* 2nd ed., vol. 4 (Oxford: Clarendon Press, 1989), p. 802.
87. *Post v. State,* 715 P.2d 1105 (Okla. Cr. 1986), *reh'g denied,* 717 P.2d 1151 (1986), *cert. denied,* 479 U.S. 890 (1986).
88. 405 U.S. 438 (1972).
89. 431 U.S. 678 (1977).
90. Thomas C. Grey, "Eros, Civilization, and the Burger Court," *Law and Contemporary Problems,* 43 (Summer 1980), 83, 90.
91. See Redlich, "Are There 'Certain Rights . . . Retained by the People'?" pp. 810–812.
92. See David A. Richards, *Toleration and the Constitution* (New York: Oxford University Press, 1986), pp. 232–233.
93. Ibid. See also Kenneth L. Karst, "The Freedom of Intimate Association," *Yale Law Journal,* 89 (March 1980), 624, 667–673.
94. See Laurence Tribe, *Abortion: The Clash of Absolutes* (New York: W. W. Norton, 1990).
95. See, e.g., John Hart Ely, "The Wages of Crying Wolf: A Comment on *Roe v. Wade,*" *Yale Law Journal,* 82 (April 1973), 920, 927–937.
96. *Skinner v. Oklahoma,* 316 U.S. 535 (1942) (sterilization); *Eisenstadt v. Baird,* 405 U.S. 438 (1972); *Griswold v. Connecticut,* 381 U.S. 479 (1965) (contraception).
97. Amend. XIV, § 1 (emphasis added).
98. See Tribe, *Abortion: The Clash of Absolutes,* pp. 129–135.
99. Erik S. Jaffe, "'She's Got Bette Davis['s] Eyes': Assessing the Noncon-

sensual Removal of Cadaver Organs under the Takings and Due Process Clauses," *Columbia Law Review,* 90 (March 1990), 528.

100. See Tribe, *Abortion: The Clash of Absolutes,* p. 110.

101. See Frank I. Michelman, "The Supreme Court, 1985 Term: Foreword: Traces of Self Government," *Harvard Law Review,* 100 (November 1986), 4.

3. Judicial Value Choice in the Definition of Rights

1. *Lochner v. New York,* 198 U.S. 45, 75 (1905) (Holmes, J., dissenting).
2. See *West Coast Hotel v. Parrish,* 300 U.S. 379 (1937).
3. See *Ferguson v. Skrupa,* 372 U.S. 726 (1963); *Williams v. Lee Optical of Oklahoma,* 348 U.S. 483 (1955).
4. See Laurence Tribe, *American Constitutional Law,* 2nd ed. (Mineola, N.Y.: Foundation Press, 1988), § 8-7, pp. 581–586.
5. *United States v. Carolene Products Co.,* 304 U.S. 144, 152–153 n.4 (1938).
6. Robert Bork, *The Tempting of America* (New York: The Free Press, 1989), p. 61.
7. See, e.g., Joseph Singer, "The Player and the Cards: Nihilism and Legal Theory," *Yale Law Journal,* 94 (November 1984), 1, 43.
8. David M. Trubek, "Where the Action Is: Critical Legal Studies and Empiricism," *Stanford Law Review,* 36 (January 1984), 575, 609.
9. *Moore v. City of East Cleveland, Ohio,* 431 U.S. 494, 503 (1977).
10. Bork, *The Tempting of America,* p. 118.
11. Ibid.
12. 482 U.S. 569 (1987).
13. See Herbert Wechsler, "Toward Neutral Principles of Constitutional Law," *Harvard Law Review,* 73 (November 1959), 1.
14. See, e.g., Bork, *The Tempting of America,* pp. 143–160; Edwin Meese, "Toward a Jurisprudence of Original Intention," *Benchmark,* 2 (1986), 1; Raoul Berger, *Government by Judiciary: The Transformation of the Fourteenth Amendment* (Cambridge, Mass.: Harvard University Press, 1977).
15. 750 F.2d 970 (D.C. Cir. 1984) (en banc), *cert. denied,* 471 U.S. 1127 (1985).
16. Ibid., p. 995.
17. Ibid.
18. See, e.g., Morris Cohen, "Property and Sovereignty," *Cornell Law Quarterly,* 13 (December 1927), 8; Felix Cohen, "Transcendental Nonsense and the Functional Approach," *Columbia Law Review,* 35 (June 1935), 809.
19. See John Locke, *Two Treatises of Government,* ed. Peter Laslett (New York: Cambridge University Press, 1988).

20. Richard Fallon, "A Constructivist Coherence Theory of Constitutional Interpretation," *Harvard Law Review,* 100 (April 1987), 1189, 1189–90. See also Philip Bobbitt, *Constitutional Fate* (New York: Oxford University Press, 1982).

21. *United States v. Carolene Products Co.,* 304 U.S. 144, 152–153 n.4 (1938).

22. *Pierce v. Society of Sisters,* 268 U.S. 510 (1925); *Meyer v. Nebraska,* 262 U.S. 390 (1923).

23. See generally Frederick Schauer, "Precedent," *Stanford Law Review,* 39 (February 1987), 57; Henry Monaghan, "Our Perfect Constitution," *New York University Law Review,* 56 (May-June 1981), 353, 387–391. Ronald Dworkin, *Taking Rights Seriously,* rev. ed. (Cambridge, Mass.: Harvard University Press, 1978), p. 38.

24. Compare *West Virginia State Bd. of Educ. v. Barnette,* 319 U.S. 624 (1943), with *Minersville School Dist. v. Gobitis,* 310 U.S. 586 (1940).

25. Bruce A. Ackerman, "The Storrs Lectures: Discovering the Constitution," *Yale Law Journal,* 93 (May 1984), 1013, 1056; B. Ackerman, *Reconstructing American Law* (Cambridge, Mass.: Harvard University Press, 1984). See also Robert Nagel, *Constitutional Cultures: The Mentality and Consequences of Judicial Review* (Berkeley: University of California Press, 1989).

26. See, e.g., *Sosna v. Iowa,* 419 U.S. 393 (1975); *Loving v. Virginia,* 388 U.S. 1, 12–13 (1967).

27. See, e.g., *Moore v. City of East Cleveland, Ohio,* 431 U.S. 494 (1977); *Griswold v. Connecticut,* 381 U.S. 479 (1965).

28. E.g., *Austin v. Michigan Chamber of Commerce,* 110 S. Ct. 1391 (1990).

29. Gerald Gunther, "The Supreme Court, 1971 Term—Foreword: In Search of Evolving Doctrine on a Changing Court: A Model for Newer Equal Protection," *Harvard Law Review,* 86 (November 1972), 1, 8.

30. 109 S. Ct. 2333 (1989).

31. Ibid., p. 2344 n.6.

32. 478 U.S. 186 (1986).

33. Ibid., p. 190.

34. Ibid., p. 199 (Blackmun, J., dissenting) (quoting *Olmstead v. United States,* 277 U.S. 438, 478 (1928) (Brandeis, J., dissenting)).

35. Jed Rubenfeld, "The Right of Privacy," *Harvard Law Review,* 102 (February 1989), 737, 749.

36. Ibid.

37. *Hardwick,* 478 U.S., p. 190.

38. 321 U.S. 158 (1944).

39. *Hardwick,* 478 U.S., p. 190.

40. 316 U.S. 535 (1942).

41. *Hardwick,* 478 U.S., p. 190.
42. Ibid.
43. 405 U.S. 438 (1972).
44. *Hardwick,* 478 U.S., p. 190.
45. Ibid.
46. Ibid.
47. Ibid., p. 206 (Blackmun, J., dissenting).
48. 367 U.S. 497 (1961).
49. Ibid., p. 543 (Harlan, J., dissenting).
50. 336 U.S. 77 (1949).
51. Ibid., p. 97.
52. 453 U.S. 490 (1981).
53. Ibid., p. 501 (plurality opinion).
54. Paul Brest, "The Fundamental Rights Controversy: The Essential Contradictions of Normative Constitutional Scholarship," *Yale Law Journal,* 90 (April 1981), 1063, 1085. See also Tribe, *American Constitutional Law,* pp. 1427–28.
55. Brest, "The Fundamental Rights Controversy," p. 1084.
56. 347 U.S. 483 (1954).
57. Brest, "The Fundamental Rights Controversy," pp. 1090–92. See also Gene R. Nichol, Jr., "Book Review: Bork's Dilemma," *Virginia Law Review,* 76 (March 1990), 337, 344–346.
58. Bork, *The Tempting of America,* p. 150.
59. Bruce A. Ackerman, "Book Review: Robert Bork's Grand Inquisition," *Yale Law Journal,* 99 (April 1990), 1419, 1422–25.

4. Seeking Guidance from Other Disciplines

1. See "How Law Is Like Literature," in Ronald Dworkin, *A Matter of Principle* (Cambridge, Mass.: Harvard University Press, 1985), pp. 146–166.
2. Compare James Boyd White, "Book Review: What Can a Lawyer Learn from Literature?" *Harvard Law Review,* 102 (June 1989), 2014, with Richard Posner, *Law and Literature: A Misunderstood Relation* (Cambridge, Mass.: Harvard University Press, 1988). See generally Robin West, "Book Review Exchange: Law, Literature, and the Celebration of Authority," *Northwestern University Law Review,* 83 (Summer 1989), 977.
3. See Anny Sadrin, *Great Expectations* (Boston: Unwin Critical Library, 1988), p. 10.
4. Ibid., p. 179.

5. See generally Ludwig Wittgenstein, *Philosophical Investigations*, 3rd ed., trans. G. E. M. Anscombe (New York: Macmillan, 1958).

6. See *Eisenstadt v. Baird*, 405 U.S. 438 (1972); *Griswold v. Connecticut*, 381 U.S. 479 (1965).

7. 381 U.S., pp. 502–503.

8. 410 U.S., pp. 221–223.

9. But see James Joyce, *Finnegan's Wake* (New York: Viking Press, 1939).

10. 476 U.S. 747 (1986).

11. Ibid., p. 776 (Stevens, J., concurring).

12. See Richard Weisman, *Witchcraft, Magic, and Religion in Seventeenth Century Massachusetts* (Amherst: University of Massachusetts Press, 1984), p. 15 and n.48.

13. See, e.g., Philip Roth, *The Facts: A Novelist's Autobiography* (New York: Farrar, Straus and Giroux, 1988).

14. Imre Lakatos, *Proofs and Refutations: The Logic of Mathematical Discovery* (New York: Cambridge University Press, 1976).

15. See Robert Fisher, *The Logic of Economic Discovery* (Brighton, Sussex: Wheatsheaf Books, 1986).

16. 392 U.S. 83 (1968).

17. Ibid., p. 102.

18. 454 U.S. 464 (1982).

19. Ibid., p. 480.

20. Lakatos, *Proofs and Refutations*, p. 15.

21. 108 S. Ct. 2597 (1988).

22. See *Myers v. United States*, 272 U.S. 52 (1926); *Humphrey's Exec'r v. United States*, 295 U.S. 602, 629 (1935).

23. *Morrison*, 108 S. Ct., p. 2619.

24. 110 S. Ct. 1595 (1990).

25. Ibid., p. 1600.

26. 319 U.S. 624 (1943).

27. 374 U.S. 398 (1963).

28. See *Hobbie v. Unemployment Appeals Commission*, 107 S. Ct. 1046 (1987). See also *Thomas v. Review Board*, 450 U.S. 707 (1981).

29. 406 U.S. 205 (1972).

30. 110 S. Ct., p. 1601 (citations omitted).

31. See, e.g., *Michael H. v. Gerald D.*, 109 S. Ct. 2333 (1989).

32. 406 U.S., p. 214.

33. 110 S. Ct., p. 1610 (O'Connor, J., concurring in the judgment).

34. *Hardwick*, 478 U.S., p. 197 (Burger, C.J., concurring).

35. See Laurence Tribe, "Trial by Mathematics: Precision and Ritual in the Legal Process," *Harvard Law Review*, 84 (April 1971), 1329.

5. Reconstructing the Constitution as a Reader's Guide

1. 109 S. Ct. 2333 (1989).
2. Ibid., p. 2352 (Brennan, J., dissenting).
3. Ibid., p. 2344, n.6 (opinion of Scalia, J., joined by Rehnquist, C.J.).
4. See *United States v. Carolene Products Co.*, 304 U.S. 144, 152–153 n.4; J. M. Balkin, "The Footnote," *Northwestern University Law Review*, 83 (1989), 275.
5. 431 U.S. 494, 503 (1977) (opinion of Powell, J.).
6. *Michael H.*, 109 S. Ct., p. 2349 (Brennan, J., dissenting).
7. See, e.g., *County of Allegheny v. ACLU Greater Pittsburgh Chapter*, 109 S. Ct. 3086 (1989); *Lynch v. Donnelly*, 465 U.S. 668 (1984).
8. See Laurence Tribe, *American Constitutional Law*, 2nd ed. (Mineola, N.Y.: Foundation Press, 1988), p. 1161 n.25.
9. See *Everson v. Board of Education*, 330 U.S. 1, 11–13 (1947).
10. *Walz v. Tax Commission of New York City*, 397 U.S. 664, 678 (1970).
11. See generally Bernard Bailyn, *The Ideological Origins of the American Revolution* (Cambridge, Mass.: Harvard University Press, 1967), pp. 246–272.
12. William McLoughlin, "Isaac Backus and the Separation of Church and State in America," *American Historical Review*, 73 (June 1968), 1392, 1413.
13. Ibid., p. 1400.
14. See Antonin Scalia, "Originalism: The Lesser Evil," *University of Cincinnati Law Review*, 57 (1989), 849, 856–857.
15. Ibid., p. 862.
16. Ibid., p. 861.
17. *Bendix Autolite Corp. v. Midwest Enterprise, Inc.*, 108 S. Ct. 2218, 2223 (1988) (Scalia, J., concurring in the judgment).
18. *Michael H.*, 109 S. Ct., p. 2344 n.6.
19. 410 U.S., pp. 129–141.
20. 405 U.S. 438 (1972).
21. *Michael H.*, 109 S. Ct., p. 2344 n.6.
22. See ibid., pp. 2337–38.
23. 110 S. Ct. 2841 (1990).
24. Ibid., p. 2859 (Scalia, J., concurring).
25. Ibid., p. 2859.
26. Ibid., p. 2863.
27. See *Garcia v. San Antonio Metropolitan Transit Auth.*, 469 U.S. 528, 564–567 and n.8 (1985) (Powell, J., joined by Burger, C.J., and Rehnquist and O'Connor, JJ., dissenting).

28. But note Justice Scalia's vote with the Supreme Court majority striking down flag-burning laws. *Texas v. Johnson,* 109 S. Ct. 2533 (1989); *United States v. Eichman,* 110 S. Ct. 2404 (1990).

29. But see Cass Sunstein, "Sexual Orientation and the Constitution: A Note on the Relationship between Due Process and Equal Protection," *University of Chicago Law Review,* 55 (Fall 1988), 1161.

30. William J. Brennan, "The Constitution of the United States: Contemporary Ratification," *University of California at Davis Law Review,* 19 (1985), 2, 4.

31. 109 S. Ct., p. 2342 n.4 (Scalia, J., joined by Rehnquist, C.J., O'Connor, J., and Kennedy, J.).

32. Laurence Tribe, *Abortion: The Clash of Absolutes* (New York: W. W. Norton, 1990), p. 97.

33. 476 U.S. 747, 792–793 n.2 (1986) (White, J., dissenting).

34. 376 U.S. 254 (1964).

35. 367 U.S. 643 (1961).

36. *Cleburne v. Cleburne Living Center, Inc.,* 473 U.S. 432, 451 (Stevens, J., concurring) (1984).

37. See, e.g., *Bendix Autolite Corp. v. Midwest Enterprise, Inc.,* 108 S. Ct. 2218, 2223 (1988) (Scalia, J., concurring in the judgment).

38. Benjamin Cardozo, *The Nature of the Judicial Process* (New Haven, Conn.: Yale University Press, 1921), p. 51.

39. Ronald Dworkin, *Law's Empire* (Cambridge, Mass.: Harvard University Press, 1986), pp. 387–389.

40. Robert Bork, *The Tempting of America* (New York: The Free Press, 1989), p. 204.

41. Laurence Tribe, *American Constitutional Law,* 1st ed. (Mineola, N.Y.: Foundation Press, 1978), p. 946.

42. 109 S. Ct., pp. 2353, 2355–59.

43. 381 U.S. 479 (1965).

44. Ibid.

45. Ibid.

46. See Gottlob Frege, "On Sense and Nominatum," trans. Herbert Feigl, in Herbert Feigl and Wilfrid Sellars, *Readings in Philosophical Analysis* (New York: Appleton-Century-Crofts, 1949), p. 86; Ludwig Wittgenstein, *Philosophical Investigations,* 3rd. ed., trans. G. E. M. Anscombe (New York: Macmillan, 1958), § 79.

47. See Saul Kripke, *Naming and Necessity* (Cambridge, Mass.: Harvard University Press, 1980).

48. See ibid., pp. 38–70.

49. *Thornburgh,* 476 U.S., p. 772 (emphasis added).

50. See Michael Seidman, "Public Principle and Private Choice: The Uneasy

Case for a Boundary Maintenance Theory of Constitutional Law," *Yale Law Journal,* 96 (April 1987), 1006.

51. Charles Black, "On Reading and Using the Ninth Amendment," in Black, *The Humane Imagination* (Woodbridge, Conn.: Ox Bow Press, 1986), p. 194.
52. Sunstein, "Sexual Orientation and the Constitution."
53. 347 U.S. 497 (1954).
54. 347 U.S. 483.
55. 347 U.S., p. 500.

Index of Cases

General Index

Ackerman, Bruce, 24, 72, 80
Arrow, Kenneth, 29
Article I: Bill of Attainder clause in, 33–34; Commerce Clause of, 39–40, 42
Article III, 91
Article IV: Republican Form Clause of, 44–45, 50–51; Privileges and Immunities Clause of, 53
Article VI: Supremacy Clause of, 83
Autonomy, state, 38–45

Bailyn, Bernard, 133n11
Balkin, J. M., 133n4
Bell, Derrick, 124n44
Berger, Raoul, 10, 129n14
Bill of Attainder clause, Article I, 33–34
Bill of Rights, 6, 53–54, 68. *See also* Rights, unenumerated
Black, Charles, 43, 115
Blackmun, Justice H. A.: dissent in *Arcara* of, 37; on states' sovereignty, 42; on fundamental right in *Hardwick*, 74
Bobbitt, Philip, 130n20
Bork, Robert H.: nomination to the Supreme Court, 3; on interpretation by Supreme Court, 51, 66–68; on Privileges and Immunities Clause, 53; on judicial value judgment, 66–67, 69; on Bill of Rights interpretation, 68; on level of generality, 80; on original understanding, 80

Brennan, Justice W. J., 12; on death penalty, 21; on Tenth Amendment, 22–23; dissent in *Arcara*, 37; on fundamental rights, 97; on meaning of tradition, 99; dissent in *Michael H.*, 103–104; on original intent, 106
Brest, Paul, 12, 79–80, 125n62
Bronner, Ethan, 121n9
Burger, Chief Justice W. E.: interpretation of Fifth Amendment by, 21; opinion in *Arcara*, 36; interpretation of Ninth Amendment by, 55
Burt, Robert, 7

Cardozo, Justice Benjamin, 109, 134n38
Chapman, John, 123n35
Choper, Jesse, 27–28, 57
Cohen, Felix, 129n18
Cohen, Morris, 129n18
Commerce Clause, 39–40, 42
Constitution: basis for interpretation, 8–13; hyper-integration concept of, 20, 24–30, 31, 33; dis-integration concept of interpreting, 20–23, 31, 33; as political theory, 28–29
Cover, Robert, 7

Declaration of Independence, 8–9
Dis-integration concept, 20–23, 31, 33
Due Process Clause, 48–49, 51–52, 104–106. *See also* Substantive due process doctrine